PIMA INDIAN LEGENDS

Illustrations by Matt Tashquinth

PIMA
INDIAN
LEGENDS

Anna Moore Shaw

THE UNIVERSITY OF ARIZONA PRESS
Tucson

About the Author . . .

ANNA MOORE SHAW, herself a Pima, began writing down these legends in 1930 when she realized they would someday be lost otherwise. Born "in the shadow of the Estrella Mountains in a lowly place among the bushes," she lived on the Pima reservations or in nearby Phoenix. Among her most interesting memories was helping to nurse the renowned Dr. Carlos Montezuma, an Apache who became a prominent surgeon in Chicago but returned later to Arizona when his health failed. Active in both tribal and non-tribal affairs, Mrs. Shaw was an ordained elder of the Salt River United Presbyterian Church, had served on the board of trustees of the C. H. Cook Christian Training School in Tempe, Arizona, and on the Salt River Reservation Mutual Self-Help Housing Commission, and for several years she edited the Salt River Pima monthly *Tribal Newsletter.*

THE UNIVERSITY OF ARIZONA PRESS

Copyright © 1968
The Arizona Board of Regents
All Rights Reserved
Manufactured in the U.S.A.
∞ This book is printed on acid-free, archival-quality paper.

L. C. No. 68-13547
ISBN 0-8165-0186-6

This book is dedicated to All People,
both young and old,
no matter what race, color, or creed.

Acknowledgments

IN ANY BOOK there are those who graciously contribute to the writing. It is to these people that I wish to express my gratitude and give recognition.

The legends recorded here were told me by my late father, Josiah Moore I. The oft-repeated legends were most entertaining and instructive, a source of enjoyment and memories. I have fond recollections of a happy childhood, and of a patient father who told and taught me these legends.

I am indebted to Mrs. Elizabeth Sherman Moore, who was an instructor at the Phoenix Technical School, teaching the methods and techniques in "Writing for Publication," in whose classes I enjoyed studying from 1950 to 1952, following which I received my certificate of completion.

To Dr. George Walker, president emeritus of Cook Christian Training School, Tempe, Arizona, a personal friend and counselor of long standing, and a man who has been a missionary and friend to my Pima people for many years, I wish to give special acknowledgment.

The encouragement to record these legends came from an outstanding Pima-Papago spiritual leader, and with a great deal of pride and admiration I point to Dr. Roe B. Lewis, who maintained that these legends should be written down and who deemed it a worthwhile contribution to the generations to come.

Mr. William S. King, who graciously offered to write the Introduction, has been a good friend to the Indian for a long time. He understands the Pima better than any other superintendent we have had at Salt River. To him go my most special thanks for the help and encouragement he has given me and my people.

Finally, I wish to give special recognition and thanks to the others who helped make this book possible: to Mr. Victor Manuel and his daughter, Mildred Manuel, two eminent Indian musicians who were most helpful in analyzing the manuscript; to Dr. Robert A. Roessel, Jr., of the Indian Education Center, Arizona State University, for his help in getting these legends reproduced in mimeographed form; to my great-nephew, Josiah Moore II, his wife, Ione, and my daughter Adeline (Mrs. A. J. Russell), who carefully typed the manuscript; to Matt Tashquinth, a fellow Pima, for his illustrations that add so much to the book; and to Marshall Townsend, director, and Kit Scheifele, editor, of the University of Arizona Press for their assistance, encouragement, and editorial direction.

ANNA MOORE SHAW

Salt River Reservation

Contents

Introduction

MANY OF US — even some from the Indian Southwest — assume that the cultures of at least some of our Indian neighbors have all but died out. We regret this and baffle our Indian friends by exhorting them to "preserve" that of their tradition which we see as remaining. This narrow view of Indian "culture" is usually viewed in aesthetic terms. Basket weaving, pottery making, silver work — even certain of the techniques of graphic arts taught in Government boarding schools during the 1930s — are commonly seen as just about all that is meaningful left to certain tribes. These, along with traditional dances, fragments of music and tribal legends, we feel, should be preserved at all cost. However well-intended are these salvage efforts by non-Indians, they are indeed arrogant in that they tell Indians which aspects of their lives (if any) are truly "Indian." They are also mistaken in that they assume that elements of culture can be "preserved" as one preserves the head of a buffalo through taxidermy.

But this is not an essay on the nature of culture; rather it is an introduction to a very charming collection of Pima legends. My purpose in bringing up the subject of culture at all is to suggest that this little book shows something of the process of cultural change. For these legends, learned more than sixty years ago in the then conservative Pima village of Gila Crossing, have been modified over the years as a reflection of changes in the cultural traditions of those who learned them. These changes notwithstanding, the legends remain every bit as much Pima as the versions told at the turn of the century. And the lady who has transcribed them is as much a part of the same Pima cultural tradition as were her parents, and their parents before them, who told the stories around countless fires on long winter nights.

Gila Crossing, the village in which Anna Moore Shaw, the youngest of ten brothers and sisters, was born, is located about thirty miles from the Pima Agency at the west end of the Gila River Indian Reservation. Neither her parents, nor her maternal grandparents who lived nearby in an old-style Pima grass house, spoke English. They were a close-knit family of Pima farmers, and their contact with the non-Indian world around them was minimal.

A major influence on the family was its ultimate conversion to Christianity by Presbyterian missionaries after a long period of opposition by Mrs. Shaw's father. During the childhood of the older children, however, and until Mrs. Shaw herself had already gone away to school, the major religious tradition of the family was native Pima in which the legends contained in this book played an important part.

Following young Anna's initial contact with the non-Indian world in the one-room day school at Gila Crossing, she was sent off to Government and mission boarding schools. Her education was concluded in 1920 with her being the first full-blooded Indian to graduate from Phoenix Union High School. Shortly after, she married Ross Shaw, also a member of the Pima Tribe from the nearby Salt River Reservation, who had just returned from France where he had been serving with the Arizona National Guard. Mr. Shaw found employment with the Railway Express Agency in Phoenix, where the couple settled and made their home for the next forty years.

The Shaws were one of the first Indian families to establish themselves solidly in Phoenix. They developed a wide circle of friends and Mrs. Shaw especially was active in church and civic affairs. Their three children grew up among non-Indian neighbors, although cousins and frequent visitors from both the Gila River and Salt River reservations kept them in close touch with the Indian world. A particularly stabilizing influence was Mrs. Shaw's father who lived with the family until all of the children were well along in school.

The stories contained in this book were told to her children by Mrs. Shaw and by her father, just as they had been told to her and to her brothers and sisters when she was a girl. But not in the same form. The inevitable changes that education, experience, and residence among non-Indians had on this Pima family were reflected in the manner in which the stories were told and in the ultimate forms that they assumed. For example, the earthy character of some, as they were told in the totally Pima atmosphere of turn-of-the-century Gila Crossing, was not appropriate in the changed urban environment. Whole elements were gradually dropped or reworded, especially since the stories more and more came to be told in English in which the cognate words and phrases sounded particularly out of place.

During an earlier period, the stories were used for instructional purposes by demonstrating examples of personal conduct. In the city and in the changed religious atmosphere of the family, moral teaching increasingly became a function of organized Christian religion. Likewise, telling the stories as rewards to children for learning the complexities of the old Pima kinship system, or committing certain of the traditional songs associated with the legends to memory, tended more and more to disappear.

By degrees, the stories were told to the children (and later to grandchildren) in much the way that fairy tales are told to non-Indian children. Even the grandfather accepted this change and, according to Mrs. Shaw, improvised the stories to hold the grandchildren's attention, much to their great delight. Coyote, who plays a dominant role in many Pima legends, for example, was dressed by the old gentleman in cowboy clothes with boots, spurs and a bright red necktie!

Mrs. Shaw began to record the stories in about 1930 because she sensed that they would not be transmitted by her children to their children. From time to time she would add to them, but did not think of them in terms of literature until many years later when non-Indian friends suggested that she attend an evening class in short-story writing. Some of these stories were published in mimeographed form by the Indian Education Center of Arizona State University in 1963.

The stories, as they are presented, occur in no particular sequence. Certain of them, like the "Great Flood," have been shortened greatly. In its original form the story of the flood is part of a complex cycle which took four nights to recount. Stories about the "Coyote" dominate, since these are a favorite of the writer and of her children and her grandchildren.

It is useful for readers not to think of these stories as having been translated from Pima; rather, they must be viewed as written in English by a native speaker. English "Indian" words are used; "many moons," "great spirit," "squaw," and the like. Mrs. Shaw feels that literal translations of equivalent Pima words would be meaningless and the words and phrases she has chosen are established ones which enhance the book's general Indian flavor. She also has worked to maintain a contemporary Pima character to the stories — to use her words — "like a pink thread running through the whole." As one who was closely associated with members of the Tribe from April, 1961, until April, 1968, I can attest that she has been quite successful in this effort.

BILL KING

Washington, D. C.

The Great Flood

ONE NIGHT many, many years ago, in the Gila River Valley where many Indians lived, heavy rain began pouring down on the peaceful valley.

"Someone has displeased the gods," cried the Chief of the village.

When the squaws went to gather mesquite wood for cooking, bubbles of water would rush out from under the wood. And when the men tilled their crops water gushed forth from the broken ground to join the rivers and creeks. Soon the swollen river overflowed its banks and the people left all their worldly goods behind and ran to higher places.

In the village lived a wise man who was lovingly called Se-eh-ha (Elder Brother) because he was like an older brother, counseling and protecting the people from harm. But now, for the first time, Se-eh-ha did not know what to do when disaster came so suddenly.

"The gods are angry! The flood is still rising. We will all perish if we do not seek refuge on the mountains," cried Se-eh-ha.

Upon hearing their elder brother's warning, the people ran to the nearby mountains. Some ran to Slanting Mountain (Superstition Mountain). They huddled on top of the highest point and cried, "Great Spirit, have pity on us and stop the flood."

When they saw the angry waters lapping on the sides of Slanting Mountain, ready to swallow them up, they turned into rocks, so frightened were they!

Now Se-eh-ha and his brother Juvet-Makai (Earth Medicine Man) were hurriedly making canoes. Coyote leisurely came by and asked, "My brothers, why are you making canoes?"

"Coyote, have you not seen the flood still rising?" said Se-eh-ha. "You had better make a canoe, else you'll drown," warned Se-eh-ha, climbing into his olla canoe. Juvet-Makai climbed into his canoe made from birds' soft down.

"Se-eh-ha, you know I also have magic power," Coyote replied. "I can use my bamboo flute for a canoe. By making myself small it will be easy to crawl into it. I'll be safer than any of you," he boasted, carelessly playing a weird melody. But when he saw the angry water rushing directly at him, he stopped playing and hastily crawled into the bamboo flute.

Se-eh-ha, Juvet-Makai, and Coyote were tossed violently by the water in different directions. Some of the birds such as the swallow, buzzard, raven, oriole, and the little hummingbird flew up to the sky to escape the great flood. They clung to the sky-ceiling with their bills. The flood reached the birds' tails, causing them to be drenched and to remain drenched-looking for all time.

The great flood lasted four days and four nights.

When at last the flood went down, Coyote, safe in his bamboo flute, was wedged on top of a high mountain near the Red River (Colorado River). He climbed out and blew on his bamboo flute to let Se-eh-ha know where he was. Since the flute was tightly stuck among the heavy rocks, Coyote left it and went to look for Se-eh-ha and Juvet-Makai.

When Coyote reached Slanting Mountain he found Se-eh-ha and Juvet-Makai standing on a big rock looking over the land.

"Coyote," Se-eh-ha wailed, "we're the only ones alive from the flood. All the inhabitants have perished. It is such a desolate place!"

After discussing their situation, Se-eh-ha declared, "Something must be done. This valley will once more laugh and sing. And we are the ones to do it!"

The Creation

SE-EH-HA (Elder Brother) gazed at the lonely place and cried, "The flood has wiped away our people. Something must be done."

Elder Brother rolled dust from his chest and threw it on the wet ground. Soon little ants formed from the dust and began making their nests. The ants minced and scattered the ground, making it partially dry.

"This is what I want the ants to do, make the ground dry," said Elder Brother, sitting down on the dry spot of ground. Earth Medicine Man and Coyote sat down too and began to make images to replace the people who had perished in the flood.

Earth Medicine Man made his images very different from the others. When Elder Brother saw the images made by Earth Medicine Man he scolded him.

"How do you expect the images to make a living with only one leg and one arm?"

Earth Medicine Man became angry and flung his images away. Without a word he sank into the ground, to find a place for himself on the other side of the earth.

When Elder Brother and Coyote finished making their images, they carefully placed them in a hastily made mud hut and built a small fire in the center of the room to keep the images warm. Every day Elder Brother and Coyote listened to discover whose images would be the first to speak.

Early one morning they heard laughter coming from the mud hut. Elder Brother and Coyote ran to see whose images were showing signs of life. They found the laughter came from Coyote's creations. It made Elder Brother very disappointed, and he took some cold water in his cupped hand and sprinkled it on Coyote's images.

"I did not want Coyote's creations to be the first to speak. Hereafter you shall be named Apaches and will always live in the north where it is cold," said Elder Brother, gathering them and throwing them to the north.

Coyote was hurt and very angry. He used his magic power and disappeared into the ground, just as Earth Medicine Man had done before him.

Elder Brother was left all alone to take care of his creations. After four days the images were talking and laughing. It made Elder Brother happy, and he named them the Aki-mal-Aatom — the River People.

The children grew under the leadership of their maker. They sang, played games, and were healthy. Once again the Gila Valley was filled with the sounds of people.

When the children reached adulthood they seriously began to farm the fertile land and rear their families. Everything went along peacefully until one day Elder

5

Brother became sick with greed and evil. Because he was their maker, he reasoned, he had the right to do as he pleased with the people. But they opposed him and eventually became his enemies.

Elder Brother went to Greasy Mountain where he made his home. There was a spring near the big Gila River in which Elder Brother used to bathe and renew his youth. He believed in the power of the spring to save him, so he was not afraid of the people.

When Elder Brother started to pay too much attention to the beautiful maidens, the people rose up in arms against him. They tried various ways to put him to death, but Elder Brother would only laugh at them and walk away. One time the people killed him, ground up his bones, and threw them in the fire to burn. Elder Brother jumped out of the fire laughing, and walked away.

The Chief and the people were helpless. Some suggested they ask Buzzard to help them. When Buzzard came, he told them he could fly to Sun and ask him. "He'll know what to do."

Buzzard flew to the Sun and laid the people's trouble before him.

"I'll give you a weapon, Buzzard. But you must go with me on my trip so I'll be able to help you," said Sun.

The next day Sun and Buzzard traveled side by side on their way to destroy Elder Brother. When they came near the Gila Valley, Buzzard used the weapon given to him by Sun. It boomed like thunder. The people heard the loud noise and were relieved, for Elder Brother was going to be put away at last.

Elder Brother also knew Buzzard and Sun were on their way to kill him.

"I'm not afraid. My spring will save me. Buzzard will get it from *me*. I will scalp him so badly he'll remain that way for all time — with a red head," said Elder Brother.

When Sun and Buzzard came over, Elder Brother heard the bang, bang, bang, and he ran to his spring and jumped in — only to be scalded. The people of the village came, and found Elder Brother's body floating in the boiling water. When the water cooled off, they pulled the body out and laid it on the shore.

The children used Elder Brother as a diving board, climbing on his back and jumping into the water. They were not afraid any more.

On the fourth day, the children again came to swim. They were surprised to see Elder Brother sitting up and driving little short sticks into the ground. After muttering mysterious words, Elder Brother sank into the ground right before the children's eyes. The frightened children ran home and told the people of what they had seen.

"Elder Brother is going down below to join Earth Medicine Man and Coyote," said the oldest man of the village. The people once again lived in fear of what Elder Brother might do to them.

Se-eh-ha Conquers the River People

AFTER SE-EH-HA MYSTERIOUSLY DISAPPEARED down into the ground, mumbling angry words, the Aki-mal-Aatom (River People) lived in fear and anxiety. Their efforts to destroy Se-eh-ha for his wrong deeds had again been futile.

"He's going down to join his brother Juvet-Makai (Earth Medicine Man). They will come and wage war against us," warned See-van Vah-Ki, a man who possessed great ability to foresee the future. He called on one of his runners, requesting him to go at once to the Big House (now called Casa Grande Ruins) some twenty-five miles away. "Ask See-van of the Big House, does his little magic stone reveal the great disaster that will soon come to our people?"

The young brave quickly threw his *wee-chi-da* ball (racing ball) on the ground, gave it a graceful kick straight ahead, and was on his way to the Big House.

With the ball to give him an even pace, running and lightly kicking it ahead of him, the runner soon reached his destination. He went straight to See-van of the Big House.

"Young brave, what is your mission?" asked See-van, smiling down at the runner.

"See-van Vah-ki is troubled deeply. He asked does your magic stone show a great disaster will soon come to our people?"

"No," answered See-van, looking out into the distance. "Tell See-van Vah-ki I see rainbows on the walls of my Big House. It is a sign the gods are pleased. They will send rains for our crops, and our people will live in plenty." The runner departed for home with the message.

In the meantime, on the other side of the earth, Se-eh-ha had been received with a warm welcome by his brother Earth Medicine Man and his friend Coyote. They sensed that Se-eh-ha's unexpected visit was due to some grave reason. After the evening meal Se-eh-ha came to the point. "My brother, Earth Medicine Man, I've come to ask you to help me. My own people have turned against me and have even tried to destroy me."

"My elder brother, Se-eh-ha, how can I help you? Your home is so far away. Besides, your people must have had a reason for turning against you," said Earth Medicine Man.

"Aw, let's help Se-eh-ha. Let's start at once," begged Coyote, a lover of excitement.

"Assemble your people and we will go up and drive out the River People. Then your people will receive their fertile lands," said Se-eh-ha.

"Your words are very good, but the counselors must be consulted. The people must be informed also." Earth Medicine Man turned to Coyote, who was waiting. "Coyote, go tell the counselors to come" But Coyote was already on his way.

Before long, Coyote returned with the counselors who stared at the visitor with questioning eyes.

Earth Medicine Man motioned for the counselors to sit down. With an air of importance Earth Medicine Man stood up and explained, "My counselors, this is my elder brother, Se-eh-ha. He came from his home on the other side of the earth and has an important matter to put before you."

Se-eh-ha glanced at the counselors, and wondered to himself, "Will they agree to my plan?" Slowly and cautiously he told about the fertile valley, about how his people abused him and even tried to kill him. "I've come to ask you to help me drive out the ungrateful River People."

The counselors said not a word, for they were too astonished. Finally the chief spokesman asked, "What reward will our people get for their work?"

"Your people will receive rich farm lands for their very own. You will be happier up there," answered Se-eh-ha, looking encouraged.

"Counselors, do you agree to my brother's plan?" asked Earth Medicine Man, scanning the faces of his men. The men talked in low tones among themselves for some time. Then one by one each counselor stood up and in a loud voice answered, "I agree."

Earth Medicine Man set the day when all the people would gather in the tribal meeting place to hear Se-eh-ha's plan.

It was early the next day. The people quickly came, for they were anxious to hear the stranger's words. Coyote, who was eager to go on the warpath, made his way among the mob, whispering to them, "It is *sä-peh*" ("It is good"). He wanted the people to agree to Se-eh-ha's plan.

Earth Medicine Man stood before the throng with arms folded. Se-eh-ha stood at his side. "This man is my elder brother, Se-eh-ha. He has a plan that will change your lives. The counselors found the matter most satisfactory, but it is for you to decide."

Se-eh-ha immediately laid his plan before the people, pointing out the many good things that would come to them after they had driven out the River People. "Your children will be well fed because the valley is rich and waiting for all kinds of seeds to be planted."

Upon hearing Se-eh-ha's words the people grunted their approval, "Ugh, it is *sä-peh* — it is good."

"Of course it is *sä-peh*. We'll show the River People a thing or two," growled Coyote.

The people wasted no time getting ready for their long journey to conquer the River People. They gathered up their belongings. The women loaded their *kia-has* (burden baskets) with food, water-filled gourds, a few personal articles such as herbs for medicine, and beads and feathers for ceremonial purposes. They must leave room in the *kia-has* for the children. Young legs tired easily, while the legs of a *kia-ha* never tired at all. The warriors went through a sham battle and used their weapons skillfully. The old men sang the war songs with the help of the women and children. Se-eh-ha smiled with great satisfaction. His plan to punish the River People was going to be accomplished.

When everyone was ready, Se-eh-ha gave his final orders. "The earth's entrance is now open. I don't want anyone to look back until all the people have marched through. Nothing must happen to hinder our journey."

Coyote's usual curiosity was aroused even more upon

hearing Se-eh-ha's orders. "I must not miss the sight!" he said, smiling mischievously.

Se-eh-ha and Earth Medicine Man proudly led the procession through the earth's entrance. The warriors followed, dressed in their tribal costumes, their faces and bodies painted with war paint, their quivers full of arrows slung over their shoulders, and their bows in their hands. The squaws and the older men whose fighting days were over busied themselves looking after the children, who were excitedly running here and there.

When he was at last above the ground, and the people were engrossed in singing their war songs, Coyote quickly looked back. The sight proved too much for him. "Look at the *kia-has* walking with their loads. The earth's entrance is like the witch Myme-wasi's cave!" Coyote's shouts were heard by Se-eh-ha, who angrily halted the march, elbowed his way through the crowd, and when he found Coyote, roughly shook him.

"Coyote, you mischievous fellow! Your disobedience has caused great harm. The *kia-has* will not walk any more, and the entrance is closed forever."

With downcast eyes Coyote wailed, "Se-eh-ha, my heart is heavy. I will obey your orders from now on." And he hit his chest with his fist to show he meant every word.

The squaws reluctantly picked up the *kia-has* to carry them on their backs. The people were separated from their kinfolk on the other side for always. Se-he-ha in a quivering voice shouted, "Those of you who are on the other side, do not weep. You will not be forgotten. As long as the sun rises and sets, a bond of *pe-cul-tha-lick* [love] will bind you to your people, though the distance divides you." It was the first trial the people had faced, but after encouraging words from their leaders they continued on their journey.

The people, led by Se-eh-ha and Earth Medicine Man, advanced toward the West. Because Se-eh-ha was determined to conquer the River People he told the warriors, "The homes must all be destroyed. Nothing is to remain standing."

Onward they marched, fighting and destroying. Whenever a fertile area was reached, a small number would express their wishes: "We like this place and wish to make our homes here."

Se-eh-ha's reply was, "You may settle here. Though the distance divides you from the rest of your tribesmen, nevertheless you will be related."

After days of traveling, the band of warriors reached the Big House we now call Casa Grande Ruins. The people there were unprepared for battle because their medicine man, See-van, had misinterpreted the many bad omens. Some of the warriors were out in the fields along the Gila River and others were away on a rabbit hunt. Only a few braves were there to defend their Casa Grande.

A large monster, Nu-big, guarded the gate. Once the monster had been a gentle little pet, but it grew to a large size. See-van kept him tied to the gate to guard the place. The monster bellowed like a bull and his teeth were sharp; his long, flexible tail cracked like a whip. He fought the enemy warriors a hard battle, but they knew how to deal with such monsters. Their sharp, swift arrows accurately hit the eyes and the monster fell to the ground, blinded.

Since it was the toughest battle Se-eh-ha's men had fought, they left without destroying the Big House.

"That is why the Big House or Casa Grande Ruins is still standing," said Owl Ear, the storyteller.

~

After Se-eh-ha had conquered the River People at the Big House, he continued leading Juvet-Makai's people towards the setting sum. He had promised to give them rich lands where any seed would grow. This promise he must keep.

The first obstacle they met was the Red River, now known as the Colorado River. It was not only wide but very deep, swift, and muddy.

"People!" Se-eh-ha shouted, for the river was rather noisy, "gather around me. Be ready to cross the river when I say the word."

He held up his crooked cane and said, "River, stop." The river rolled back, making it safe for the people to walk across. Then the river rolled forward again.

It so happened that a young couple with a frightened child were late in getting to the river, and so were left behind.

Se-eh-ha called to them from the far side of the river, "Since you did not obey my orders, you will have to remain where you are. But you will be related to the rest of the Indians." There was nothing the young couple could do but stay and make their home on the east bank of the river. Their descendants are said to be the Cocopah Tribe.

Se-eh-ha rejoiced because he had kept his promise to the good people whom he had brought from the other side of the earth to help him subdue the ungrateful River People.

The hard task was over. Se-eh-ha was aware of the feelings of enmity of his own people. "My own do not want me. But my home in the Greasy Mountains is calling me." Se-eh-ha returned to the Gila Valley to see if his spring which was at Gila Crossing was still there. Yes, it was there, and it looked the same as it had before he left for Juvet's-Makai's land.

The Maze, or Se-eh-ha's House

AFTER SE-EH-HA RETURNED to his home in the Greasy
Mountains he decided to build a new home, a dwelling
that would be like a labyrinth with winding passages.
His purpose was to bewilder the enemy should they come
to destroy him. "I'll be safe in my lodge in the center
of my maze dwelling," he told himself.

One morning after he had finished his new home,
Se-eh-ha arose very early. The day was calm and bright,
but not the heart of Se-eh-ha. It was troubled. He sought
to ease his feelings by reminding himself, "Am I not
their Creator and Elder Brother?"

He climbed to the top of his new *ki* (house), shading
his eyes from the bright sunlight. As was his custom, he
looked towards the east. He saw a thick cloud of dust
appear on the horizon. "Ha! I know the enemy is on

15

its way to destroy me. We'll see who is more powerful!" Se-eh-ha hurriedly went back to his lodge, way down in the heart of the maze.

Before long the warriors arrived shouting their war cry. They found the entrance of the maze wide open. Never had they seen such a strange-looking dwelling. It was like the mouth of a big monster, ready to swallow anyone who entered. One by one the warriors walked in. They quickly walked through the narrow, dark, winding halls. Soon the warriors were groping their way. It was so dark! Some fell, gasping for lack of air. The winding halls were soon cluttered with warriors, stumbling and piling on top of each other.

All the while, Se-eh-ha sat smug and content in his lodge. He knew the enemy had all perished. Once again Se-eh-ha was the Conqueror.

It is told by the Old Ones that Se-eh-ha's *ki* (house) is located in the South Mountains near Phoenix, Arizona. In one of the gorges of these mountains were found an olla and a grinding stone which the Pimas believe are relics of the past and of the maze dwelling of Se-eh-ha.

Today the maze pattern is still woven into the Pima baskets. It is like the pattern of life — with obstacles to dim the way. But happy is the man who rises to the top.

The Rattlesnake Receives His Fangs

ONCE THE RATTLESNAKE was a gentle and timid little snake. His maker, the Sun God, had made him very beautiful. But he forget to give him a weapon with which to defend himself. Therefore he was the most abused and miserable little snake in the desert land of the red men.

In the evenings when the people's work was done, there would be merrymaking in the village ceremonial grounds. Sometimes there was singing, dancing, and playing of games. Other times Owl Ear, the storyteller, would recount legends of long ago.

Rattlesnake attended the gatherings because he liked to sing. But best of all he liked to hear the legends. Everything went very well with the little snake until one evening a prankster attended the merrymaking.

The prankster, whose name was Rabbit, wanted to have

some fun, so he picked up the little snake and tied him in a knot as if he were a piece of rope. With much merriment, the young braves tossed the snake back and forth over the campfire like a ball. This rough treatment went on every evening, and poor little Rattlesnake would crawl home in pain.

"I'll stay away from the meeting place," he would moan. But the whoops and the beating of the drums always upset his intentions, and Rattlesnake would again crawl to the merrymaking.

This rough treatment from the men went on and on. Rattlesnake would cry, "My bones ache and I cannot sleep."

Early one morning, after a sleepless night, Rattlesnake asked the Sun God to help him. "Have pity on me and help me!"

The Sun God answered, "I will help you. You have been badly treated, and I must put a stop to it at once." Like a flash of lightning the Sun God appeared before the ailing little snake.

"Now open your mouth wide and I will place two of my powerful rays in your upper jaw. Hereafter you are going to be the most powerful of the desert snakes. But first you must give a warning with your rattle. When your warning is not heeded, then you may strike with your sun-ray fangs."

"I will do just as you've ordered," said Rattlesnake, feeling very important.

The next evening, Rattlesnake attended the meeting. "I wonder who will be my first victim?" he thought, coiling himself in a dark corner away from the crowd. But he didn't have to wait long, for at that moment naughty Rabbit saw him and came over to have some more fun with Rattlesnake. Rabbit kicked Rattlesnake and laughed when he heard the snake's rattle.

"Are you sounding off with your rattle like the medicine man?" asked Rabbit, and again he kicked Rattlesnake. Like a flash, Rattlesnake bit him.

"My foot! My foot!" cried Rabbit, limping to one corner of the grounds to nurse his wounds.

The astonished men rushed up to see what had happened.

Owl Ear, the storyteller, defended Rattlesnake. "Rattlesnake has always been a gentle little fellow. I have watched the ill treatment of our little friend, and I must say that Rabbit has received his punishment at last."

The news of Rattlesnake's sun-ray fangs went all over the land.

Thereafter the people were afraid of Rattlesnake, whose maker had given him such powerful fangs to use for his protection.

The Legend of Eagleman

IT WAS ON A SUMMER MORNING in the days before Se-eh-ha lost the love of the River People. Just as the sun came over the eastern hills, the Chief of Cactus Village stood on his brush arbor and shouted, "My people! The gods have favored us. We have stored enough food to last all winter. Our families are well fed. Tomorrow at dawn the warriors will go on a rabbit drive. Each man must have four arrows. Get busy and repair your weapons."

The day was a busy one for the people. The men joked with one another and the village hummed with excitement. The women were busy roasting wheat, grinding it fine on their *metates* (stone grinders). *Pinole* would be good to take on the rabbit drive.

Tall Flowers, a beautiful maiden, took the children to clean gourds at the spring.

"Fill the gourds with fresh water," she said. The children all loved Tall Flowers and willingly obeyed her. Everyone worked for this special day.

Before sunrise the hunters departed for their usual hunting grounds near Ga-gautke — Slanting Mountain — or Superstition Mountain as we know it now.

Suddenly a young brave whose name was Hick-vick (Woodpecker), cried, "I have only two arrows instead of four."

"Go home and get the rest of your arrows," ordered the Chief. "We'll wait for you in the shade of this mesquite tree."

Hick-vick ran back to the village. When he reached the spring near Slanting Mountain, he stopped to get a cool drink of water. He was surprised to hear a woman's voice.

"I have some good *pinole* in this bowl. Please drink it, you look hungry." The young brave eagerly drank the *pinole*. Every swallow caused little pin feathers to come out all over his body.

"What is happening to me? I feel so strange," wailed Hick-vick. Soon he was changed into a huge eagle.

"Ha, ha, ha," laughed the old witch. "I mixed ground eagle feathers in the *pinole*. Hereafter you will be Eagle-man."

In the meantime the hunters waited for Hick-vick to return. The Chief grew impatient.

"What is keeping the boy?"

He sent a runner to find out what was detaining him.

The runner started at once. When he reached Slanting Mountain, he saw a large eagle sitting by the spring. The eagle had the head of Hick-vick but his body, wings, and talons were those of a huge eagle.

Immediately the runner returned to tell the hunters his discovery.

"Hick-vick has been changed to a big eagle. I saw an ugly old woman running to the mountain. She was carrying a bowl," related the runner.

The Chief sadly nodded his head and recalled past events. He told the young braves about the legend.

"Once the witch was a beautiful maiden. But she was proud and disobeyed her parents; the gods changed her into an ugly old witch. She lives in a cave on the side of Slanting Mountain, and now and then she comes out to bewitch someone," explained the Chief. "It means the gods are angry. Let us return to our village at once."

When they passed near the spring they found Eagleman sitting with his bow and two arrows. The hunters aimed their sharp arrows at the bird, but he deftly caught the arrows with his talons. He flew to a palo verde tree and alighted on one of the branches, which broke under his heavy body. Then he flew away. When the hunters saw this they decided there was nothing to do but to return home and warn their people.

Eagleman flew over the land until he found a big cave near the top of a high cliff. There he made his home and hunted for game to satisfy his great appetite.

When all the game was gone, Eagleman started to kill the people of Cactus Village. Those who escaped him lived in fear and anxiety.

One day Eagleman swooped down on the home of Tall Flowers and carried her away to make her his bride. The people heard her cries for help, but were powerless to help her. The village of Cactus went into mourning for their beloved daughter. The Chief and his counselors held meetings to find a way to kill Eagleman.

"He'll wipe out the whole tribe," reasoned the Chief.

Tall Flowers' uncle remembered Elder Brother, a wise old man. "He'll help us."

The next day a young runner went to the home of Elder Brother on top of Greasy Mountain (South Mountain). He returned with distressing words. "Elder Brother is not there. His house is deserted."

The people were deeply disappointed. Every so often someone would go to see if Elder Brother had returned to his house, only to find it still empty.

Finally, after a year, only a small number of the tribe remained alive in Cactus Village. A runner went again to Elder Brother's home and was relieved to find him there at last.

"Elder Brother, I've been told to come and ask you to help us," explained the runner.

"What's the trouble?" asked Elder Brother.

"Eagleman has been killing our people and we're unable to stop him."

"Go home and tell your people I'll come after four days have passed," said Elder Brother.

The runner returned to his village and told the Chief that Elder Brother would not come to their aid for another four days. It was discouraging news. During those days Eagleman made his regular raids without trouble.

At last the four days passed, and Elder Brother came to the village to give help to the people. The warriors went with Elder Brother to show him the high cliff where Eagleman lived.

When they arrived, Elder Brother took out some stakes cut from very hard wood. He drove the first stake into the side of the cliff, using his stone ax.

"Before I climb the cliff I want to ask you to return to your village and tell the people to watch my mountain home. If they see white clouds floating over Greasy Mountain, it is a sign I have killed Eagleman. But if black clouds appear you will know I've been killed by Eagleman," said Elder Brother.

Elder Brother slowly ascended the high cliff, driving the hard stakes and using them as an *isk-liff* (ladder). It was a slow, difficult climb, but Elder Brother was used to all kinds of hardships. Besides, he wanted to help the people.

When he reached the top of the cliff he found the cave, the home of Eagleman. Cautiously he peered into the dark cave, shading his eyes with his hands so as to see clearly.

A small cry came from the dark cave. It was the glad cry of Tall Flowers.

"My Elder Brother, you ought not to have come. It's risky," sobbed Tall Flowers.

"I'll risk my life to save you, Tall Flowers. Stop your crying and tell me, when does Eagleman come home?"

"He generally gets home at noon," answered Tall Flowers, drying her eyes.

They quickly decided what course of action to take, for time was running short.

"But the child will reveal your presence. He's very much like his father and takes great delight in killing the helpless little insects around here."

"Don't worry. I'll be safe." Elder Brother took some ashes from the fireplace and made a mark across the child's mouth, rendering him unintelligible. In the distance they heard a great noise like peals of thunder. Eagleman was on his way home. Elder Brother quickly changed himself into a little fly and hid under a corpse which was in one part of the cave.

When Eagleman arrived he dumped his load on top of the corpse, hiding Elder Brother more securely. His little

son ran to his father and exclaimed, "*A-pa-pa Chu-vich!*
A-pa-pa Chu-vich!"

"What is the boy trying to tell me? I command you,
Tall Flowers, to tell me."

"There is nothing to tell. No one ever comes here, as
you well know."

"But someone *is* here." Eagleman searched the cave
for any living creature but did not find anyone. He sat
down and ate his meal. Afterwards he put his head on
Tall Flowers' lap and took a nap.

Tall Flowers sang a soft lullaby, whistling after each
stanza. Eagleman heard and asked sleepily, "Why do you
sing and whistle?"

"Because I'm so happy to see you bring home plenty of
meat."

Eagleman finally went into a deep sleep and did not
hear Tall Flowers' whistle.

Elder Brother came out very quietly. With his stone ax
he gave Eagleman a hard blow on his head, killing him
instantly. The child met the same treatment. Elder
Brother knew it was not a nice thing to do, but the
people's safety was his first concern, and he wanted to
make certain of their safety forever. He cut off the eagle's
head and threw it to the east, and his body he tossed to
the west.

Tall Flowers buried her face against the cliff outside
the cave. Her heart was badly torn but she, too, felt that
the safety of her people came first. So she leaned against
the hard cliff to give her strength.

Elder Brother came out after he had made sure his task
was completed. As he started to help Tall Flowers climb
down the ladder of stakes, the cliff swayed back and forth.
Eagleman's power was felt even in death.

When the rocking of the cliff stopped, Tall Flowers

and Elder Brother descended. Her uncle welcomed her joyously and took her home.

Meanwhile, the people patiently watched the mountain home of their Elder Brother. Their hearts were glad when they saw white clouds floating over Greasy Mountain. Eagleman was destroyed at last!

Hohokam – The People Who Are Gone

CENTURIES AGO the Hohokam Indians lived in the fertile valleys of the Salt and Gila rivers.

Like any primitive people they struggled for their existence. Mother Nature taught them what desert plants were edible, what roots and herbs had medicinal value.

Their main problem was how to obtain water for their arid fields. It was then that they dug the first canals with their bare hands, sharp sticks, and stone axes. The women helped in this great enterprise, carrying the loose dirt from the canals in their baskets. When the arduous task was finished their hearts were filled with satisfaction. Their happiness was complete when they saw the life-giving water rush through the canals to water their thirsty crops. A bountiful harvest of beans, corn, cotton, melons, and pumpkins rewarded their labors.

Chief Koo-vith (Antelope) set a day of rejoicing with a feast and tribal ceremonials. Excitement mounted with anticipation of the joyous event.

The women cried, "No more hungry stomachs for our little ones. We'll roast corn and venison in the open fire pit."

They feasted, sang, and danced to the Bluebird's songs and to the beat of the tom-tom. The young braves demonstrated their skills in the use of the *ka-vat* (shield) and the bow and arrow. Raven Nest, the old storyteller, enthralled the children with myths and legends of long ago.

But peaceful days were broken by enemy tribes harassing their villages.

The counselors advised, "Something must be done. A big house must be built for the protection of our people." It took many days of back-breaking toil and blistered hands to build the Great House (Casa Grande).

~

After many centuries the ruins of Casa Grande still stand in the Arizona desert, on the banks of the once-mighty Gila River. The ruins are a monument to the noble Hohokam — "The People Who Are Gone" — whose achievements have left to all people a valuable lesson in patience and determination.

To this day some of the Pimas agree that the Hohokam were driven out by Earth Medicine Man's people.

A Potsherd Speaks

ONE DAY a small piece of broken pottery complained, "Once I was a useful olla but now I am only a little sherd."

"What is your trouble?" asked Sandstorm, who was passing by and heard the little potsherd's grumblings.

"Long ago, an Indian maiden of Hohokam land molded me into an olla and I was so proud to hold water for the braves, the women, and their children. But one day great trouble came to the Hohokam and they left their villages in haste. In her hurry, the Hohokam maiden dropped me and ran to catch up with her fleeing people. Now I am just a broken piece of pottery," cried the little sherd.

"Do not weep, little sherd, for I'm going to help you," said Sandstorm. "I'm going to cover you with a soft blanket of sand so you will not be trampled to a powder. Some day you will become useful again, just wait and see."

29

Sandstorm blew, and blew, and blew, rolling a fine layer of sand over the little sherd.

Many harvests passed and the little potsherd began to get very tired of waiting.

"Is this the end for me?" moaned the little sherd. "I'm wasting my time under a cover of sand!"

Again Sandstorm heard the little sherd's grumblings and decided it was time to do something. So Sandstorm asked Rain for help.

"But you know I'm blind, so how can I see the place where you covered the sherd?" asked Rain.

"I'll lead you to the place," said Sandstorm, "but first let me blow on my reed flute so the little sherd will know we're coming." Sandstorm began to blow softly.

Then as Sandstorm and Rain came close to where the little sherd was covered, Sandstorm gave a mighty blast, causing most of the blanket of sand to roll aside.

"Now, Rain, it's your turn. Let me see what you can do," challenged Sandstorm.

Rain fell, patter, patter, patter, all night long. In the morning Sandstorm led Rain back to his home, for their work had ended.

Soon a Pima maiden came by to get sand to mix with clay to make an olla. She found the little sherd that had been uncovered by Sandstorm and Rain the night before.

"A-yah! Oh! What a beautiful piece of Hohokam pottery," she exclaimed, taking the little sherd in her hand to study the pretty pattern. The maiden took the sherd home and skillfully copied the design on her new olla.

"I am so happy!" whispered the little sherd. "Now I am useful, and I will be a link between the Hohokam of the past and the Pimas of the present."

~

Because a sandstorm usually precedes the rain, the Pimas tell their children, "The rain is blind and always has to be led by the sandstorm."

Little Yellow Bird

EARLY ONE LATE SPRING MORNING fifteen-year-old Yellow Bird went to gather bean pods from the palo verde trees that grew near Bä-bät (Frog) Mountain in the Santa Catalina range of mountains. Her mother had begged her to wait until she could find time to go with her. Had Yellow Bird obeyed her mother, this story never would have been told.

Yellow Bird wanted to show her parents she was old enough to help bring food from the desert plants. "Have I not learned to weave mats from the yucca leaves?" she said, tossing her long black hair. Taking her mother's burden basket, Yellow Bird started on her way to the Bä-bät Mountain.

On the road she saw Whirlwind dancing and whirling towards her. She stepped aside, but Whirlwind caught her and spun her around so fast she could not get away.

"My little Yellow Bird," he said, "don't be afraid. I will take you on a ride over the mountain top." Away they went, whirling, whirling. Up, up, up. Yellow Bird could do nothing, for Whirlwind was so very strong.

When they were on the top of a high mountain, Whirlwind gently stopped and Yellow Bird jumped to the ground.

"Yellow Bird, I'll be back," said Whirlwind. "Perhaps Yellow Bird will learn to be patient," he mumbled.

Of course little Yellow Bird was very frightened. She was far away from home.

"Father! father!" she called. "I'm lost on the high mountain. Come and help me." But her father was too far away, and did not hear his daughter's cries.

When evening came, Yellow Bird had not returned home. Her parents were very alarmed. They called to their friend Nu-ee (Buzzard), the big black bird that was sitting in the tree near by.

"Nu-ee," the father cried. "We're so worried. Yellow Bird has not returned home. She took the burden basket and went to gather palo verde pods to roast for food. I found her burden basket lying in the road. An evil spirit must have taken her."

"My friend," said Nu-ee, "I will fly over all the land and search for your daughter. My eyes are very sharp. I'm sure I'll find her."

Nu-ee, the big black bird, flew over the land, but he could not find Yellow Bird.

"My heart is heavy, my friend," said Nu-ee when he returned. "I could not find your daughter. But when I passed a high mountain I heard someone crying on the mountain top."

"Nu-ee, that must have been Yellow Bird. I will ask Naf-choo to help me. He's very wise and helps everyone."

Yellow Bird's father hurried to the home of Naf-choo in a cave on the side of Bä-bät Mountain. Upon his arrival he called four times, as is the Indian custom.

"Naf-choo! Naf-choo! Naf-choo! Nafchoo!"

A pleasant voice from within answered four times, "Naf-choo! Naf-choo! Naf-choo! Naf-choo! Come in. What can I do for you?"

"My daughter Yellow Bird is lost on a high mountain. She cannot climb down," cried the father.

Naf-choo hastily put on his deerskin sandals and took a tiny pouch of wild gourd seeds. Taking his bow and arrows he started for the high mountain.

Yellow Bird's father silently followed. When they reached the foot of the high mountain they heard the maiden weeping.

Naf-choo dug the earth and planted the gourd seeds at the foot of the mountain. He sang the Pima Grow Song four times, meanwhile making gestures with his hands:

"A me voosh ne.
Has ba ki na."

By the time his chanting ended, the vines had sprouted and reached the top of the mountain.

"Maiden, climb down; the vine is very strong," called Naf-choo.

Yellow Bird climbed down the vine ladder and soon was in the arms of her father.

"My good friend Naf-choo, you are so very kind. How can I ever return your kindness!" exclaimed the happy father.

But Naf-choo, more concerned about his magic seeds,

did not answer until he had knelt down on the sandy soil and dug out his seeds. Then he answered four times, in the Indian tradition, *"Nä-vä-che"* (friend).

Yellow Bird's father returned the salutation, repeating four times, *"Nä-vä-che."*

Little Yellow Bird had learned a great lesson — to obey her parents.

The
Haughty Chief

HAWK WAS A TALL, handsome, stalwart chief of thirty-five years who lived in a Yuma Indian village near the mighty Red River (Colorado River) with his wife and their son of fourteen summers.

For many years Hawk's father had been chief of the Yuma tribe. Upon his death, his young son, also named Hawk, became chief according to their tribal custom.

The young Chief was full of energy and very anxious to show other tribes his strength and valor. Therefore, when news reached him of how the Aki-mal-Aatom (River People), Pima Indians living in the Gila Valley, were successful in defending their homes from their enemies, the young Chief boasted.

"Bah! The Pimas are not the only people who can fight! My tribe, the Yumas, can fight, too," boasted Chief Hawk, showing off the hard muscles in his arms.

Chief Hawk wasted no time assembling his braves in front of his mud-thatched house.

"My men, we are going to Pima-land and fight. We'll show them our wooden warclubs are better than their bows and arrows," explained Chief Hawk, his voice ringing with excitement.

"No! No! We must not subject our fine young braves to such a foolish plan unless it is necessary," advised Hummingbird, his chief counselor. "The Pimas are used to fighting on their ponies. They'll run us down and we'll all be trampled and killed!"

"My mind is made up. I have already asked our friends the Mohave Indians to help us. Their chief told me they will join us somewhere along the way. Go to your homes and get ready for our journey to Pima-land," ordered the haughty Chief.

At dawn a band of one hundred Yuma warriors set out on foot towards Pima-land. Their faces were painted with red and black paint, and bird feathers dangled from their heads. Their wooden clubs hung down from their belts. They joked and laughed as they walked across the endless stretch of desert. With them was the Chief's son. The young lad had accompanied his father in order to obtain experience and, best of all, the honor that is the goal of all young braves.

The sun was shining brightly and the birds twittered in the trees. The land seemed peaceful, but suddenly a cracking sound of breaking twigs attracted the attention of the warriors. They stopped and listened.

"What is it? An enemy?" they asked. Just then a lone deer ran weakly into view and dropped dead in front of them.

"It's a bad omen!" cried Hummingbird. "Our fine

young warriors will be defeated. Let us turn back and return to our village!"

"We must go on," ordered the young Chief, his eyes blazing with anger. Onward they traveled until they came to a little brook. The men were exhausted, and the clear, cool water was indeed a welcome sight.

"Fish! Fish!" shouted the Chief's son. His sharp eyes were the first to discover the school of fish in the clear water. The warriors eagerly waded into the brook with shouts and laughter, and soon caught some of the fish with their hands. There was much excitement. Hummingbird hushed their noise with words of wisdom.

"Do you see the water has turned red with blood and does not wash downstream? It is another bad sign. Chief Hawk, the gods are telling us to give up our warpath and return home at once!"

"No! We will not give up our plans. We will go on. If there are any cowards in our band, you may return to your homes at once. You will not be fit to call yourselves warriors," retorted the haughty Chief as he searched the faces of his warriors for any evidence of cowardice. "The bloody water is a sign we will be victorious," he added.

The men grumbled among themselves but decided to go along rather than become unpopular with their new Chief.

After days of hard traveling the Yuma warriors reached Gray Mountain, where they found the Mohave warriors waiting to join them. Chief Hawk's face brightened, but he was puzzled by the strangers in the group.

"And who are these men?" he asked.

"They are Mountain Indians, better known as Apaches, and bitter enemies of the Pimas," answered the Mohave Chief.

"Then we are sure to win the battle," exclaimed Chief

Hawk, bursting into the Yuma victory song, twisting his body sideways, ducking. weaving, and stamping his feet to the war chant.

"We will meet our death," muttered Hummingbird under his breath, not daring to oppose his Chief openly in the presence of the Mohaves and Apaches.

That evening a council was held to make plans for attacking the Pimas. An Apache warrior advised, "Let us attack at night when the Pimas are asleep. I've had many battles with them and I know their way of fighting. The Pimas do not give up easily; they fight to the end. If we leave at once we can get away before they get reinforcements from those Pimas living in the Upper Gila Valley."

"Yes, this Apache knows from experience," said the Mohave Chief.

"If you are such cowards, return to your homes now and put on dresses, you weaklings," shouted Chief Hawk, angrily pacing back and forth in front of the men.

For a few moments the warriors were silent. In the distance the hooting of an owl was plainly heard.

"Another sign of defeat!" advised Hummingbird. "The hooting of an owl is never a good sign. It is a sure sign of death."

"Come, my brave Yuma warriors. Nothing is going to stop us from fighting. We'll fight in broad daylight," said the haughty Chief, ignoring the words of his counselor. "We want the Pimas to see how strong and brave we are."

As a result of the Chief's angry words, the Mohave and Apache braves left the Yuma band and returned to their homes.

"Let the Yuma warriors go to meet their doom," said the wise Mohave Chief.

Eastward the Yuma braves marched under the leadership of Chief Hawk. After several days of hardship in the desert under the sweltering sun, they reached the Gila River flowing near a long mountain range. High, rugged Komatke (Flat Mountain) stood boldly in the quiet, peaceful valley.

"This is Pima-land," said Hummingbird. "I remember this high mountain. Chief Hawk, let us stop here awhile so our warriors may rest for the hard day ahead."

"Bah! Why waste time?" replied Chief Hawk impatiently.

The morning sun had just peeped over the eastern horizon on this most unforgettable day!

As the Yumas neared the first village, they met three squaws whom they recognized as Maricopas. Since their language was somewhat similar, the Yuma Chief asked, "Where are you going so early in the morning? Tell us where we may find your brave warriors."

The women were afraid and ran for safety. "We're going out to gather mesquite beans. The warriors are over there," called one of the women over her shoulder, pointing toward the first village.

Some of the Yuma warriors chased the women, who ran as fast as they could and disappeared into the dense mesquite growth.

A Maricopa warrior who had awakened early was outside tending to the baby while the mother was cooking breakfast; noticing the cloud of dust made by the invading Yuma tribe, he ran, carrying his child, to warn the nearest Pima village with shouts of "Enemy! Enemy!"

When the Pimas heard the warning, they sent a young brave on his fastest pony to relay the warning to the Pimas living further up the Gila Valley. The news spread like wildfire. It did not take long for the Maricopa and Pima warriors to come full speed on their ponies to meet the invading Yuma warriors.

The women and children ran to the nearest mountain for safety.

When the opposing tribes gathered at the place where the battle was to take place, the Pimas through the interpretation of a Maricopa warrior agreed to fight according to a plan proposed by the Yuma chief.

Two straight lines were marked on the ground about three feet apart, one by each of the opposing chiefs. Then they placed their men on the lines facing each other, the Yuma warriors with their warclubs and the Pima and Maricopa warriors, armed with bows and arrows, on their ponies. The agreement was that each force was to remain on its own side of the marked lines.

When everyone was ready, the warriors struck at each other with their weapons. The swift arrows of the Pimas and Maricopas proved too much for the Yuma warriors and one by one they fell to the ground. In the din of battle the lines were soon forgotten, and warriors were running all over the battlefield.

Soon only a handful of Yuma warriors remained. Chief Hawk bravely stood his ground with the help of his brave young son who snatched some of the flying arrows and used the bow of a fallen Pima warrior to shoot back at the Pimas.

Finally father and son fell at the hands of the Pimas whom they had come to conquer. The handful of Yumas who were left ran toward the east end of Komatke Mountain for safety, but were quickly run down by the Pima warriors on their ponies. One survivor alone escaped, and he returned home by swimming down the Gila River. He told his people about the terrible battle.

Thus did the haughty chief meet his tragic end along with his son and his noble warriors.

The Great Hunters

AT THE EDGE of an Indian village lived five brothers. Their names were Mountain Lion, Buzzard, Coyote, Raven, and Bobcat. They were skilled with the bow and arrow and had never been defeated by either friend or foe. The people of the village lovingly called them "The Great Hunters."

During the summer moons, when the days were long, the Great Hunters every day brought home deer, buffalo, mountain goat, and sometimes a rabbit. The meat was cut in thin narrow strips and hung on long cactus ribs to dry in the sun. When thoroughly dried, the meat was stored in deerskin bags and hung from the rafters for winter food. The pelts of the animals were cleaned and stored, too. The Great Hunters used these pelts in making

43

shields, quivers, and sandals for themselves and for the people of the village.

The people loved them and were very proud of the Great Hunters. But there was one person who envied them for their skill and their fame.

Old man Mist secretly watched the five brothers from his home on the mountain top.

"The Great Hunters are storing up too much meat," complained Mist. "I must not let them. I shall starve them by fencing away the wild animals where the Great Hunters cannot find them. Their fame will be ended forever."

He asked his friend Mirage to help him carry out his wicked plan.

"Get some of the young braves to build a strong corral near Crystal River," ordered the jealous Mist.

"But the braves will want some of the meat in return for their work," objected Mirage. "Besides, they will not help you if they know about your wicked plan."

"Tell them nothing of my plan," thundered Mist. "Just tell them they will get meat in return for their work."

When the corral was finished the braves helped Mirage drive all the wild animals of the mesquite forest into the large enclosure.

When the Great Hunters went out to hunt they could not find any wild game.

"What has happened to the game?" they asked one another in puzzled tones.

Each day they went to hunt, only to return home without food. The deerskin bags of food became lighter and lighter. Soon the food was all used up. Only the empty bags swung lightly from the rafters to remind them of the times of plenty.

"What shall we do? We'll starve to death if we do not

find food at once!" cried Mountain Lion, oldest and wisest of the five brothers.

"We must find food before it is too late," he wailed, glancing anxiously towards the dark corner where little brother Bobcat, feeling the pangs of hunger more than the others, was curled up, too weak to move.

But he was not too weak to speak. "Why not choose brother Buzzard to scout for food! He flies higher than any other bird of the desert. He'll find food for us," boasted Bobcat in his weak little voice.

"If there is food anywhere, Buzzard will find it," agreed the brothers.

"Brother Buzzard, you have been chosen to fly over all the land and search for food," ordered Mountain Lion.

"Not a nook or crevice will be left unsearched," promised Buzzard, flapping his wings to show he meant every word.

The next day Buzzard arose at dawn and quietly departed on his important journey. He flew over the dense mesquite forest, straining his eyes for a sign of wild game. He looked in the shade of every rock, under every bush, and along the riverbanks where the wild animals usually rested after a cool drink. But his search was futile. Buzzard shuddered at the unhappy thought of what would happen to his little brother, Bobcat, if he failed to bring food.

"But where shall I search next?" he cried in despair, tears rolling down his silky breast and rumpling his feathers.

Finally he came to a small butte surrounded by miles of woodland with a glassy river flowing nearby. He alighted wearily on a large flat rock on top of the butte. He was very hungry and discouraged. But after resting a short time Buzzard felt better.

"I must not give up," he said. With fire in his eyes he made a solemn promise. "I will not return home until I find food." His eyes rested on the land below. At that moment he saw a group of men driving a deer from a corral at the edge of the woods.

"Ho! Ho!" Buzzard exclaimed. The longer he looked on the scene below, the more certain he was of his discovery. "So all the animals have been fenced. I shall go down and find out who has played such a dirty trick."

Buzzard flew down from the butte in the direction of the corral. He must be careful not to cause any suspicion. When he was a short distance away, Buzzard could hear plainly every word coming from the corral.

"Someone is coming up the trail," said one of the men.

"What does he look like?" asked Mirage.

"He has on dark clothes and is wearing a red headdress," answered the brave.

"Let him come. He's a stranger on his way to the next village," said Mirage.

When Buzzard arrived looking very tired, hungry, and dusty, Mirage met him with some meat.

"Take this tender meat and broil it over the campfire," he said, pointing to a fire at the foot of a large boulder.

"It'll keep him busy and I can watch him from here. The braves must not be told he is one of the Great Hunters," reasoned Mirage.

But Buzzard remembered his starving brothers at home, especially little brother Bobcat, and he didn't have the heart to eat the meat. Instead he carefully wrapped the meat in his red headdress. Then he climbed on top of the boulder and pretended to take a nap. When the men were too busy again to watch him, Buzzard examined the corral out of the corners of his eyes. Every now and then Mirage

46

looked up from his work to watch Buzzard. He felt at ease to see Buzzard sound asleep.

"He looks starved and weak. He cannot open the heavy gate," thought Mirage. So he ordered the young braves, "Come! Let us start back to the village. Mist is waiting for the venison." The braves departed, taking all the meat with them.

When Mirage and his men were out of sight, Buzzard flew down from the boulder. With his claws he scraped up every bit of the dried blood from the willow mat on which the deer had been slaughtered.

"My brothers will have a good nourishing meal from this blood," said Buzzard, putting the blood in his head-dress with the venison. "It will help brother Bobcat to regain his strength." And with a light heart Buzzard departed for home.

When Buzzard arrived with his precious load, his hungry brothers rejoiced. They cheerfully called to little Bobcat, who was still curled up in the dark corner of the room.

"Brother Bobcat, wake up! Our brother Buzzard has found food for us. You'll soon be well again," said Raven, bending over Bobcat.

"I knew Buzzard would find food," said Bobcat in his weak little voice. Like the rest of the brothers he was very eager to hear about Buzzard's trip and where he had found the food. But it was not polite to ask. He must wait patiently for the right time to hear about the trip.

Afer a warm hearty meal of venison and boiled blood the five brothers sat around the campfire.

Finally Mountain Lion asked, "Brother Buzzard, you may now tell us where you found the food."

"Yes, please tell us all about your trip," said little Bob-cat, who was lively again after a good meal.

"I am glad my strength did weaken on my long journey.

Otherwise I never would have discovered the fenced animals," answered Buzzard, hugging his little brother, Bobcat, who was sitting beside him.

"What! The animals are fenced?" roared Mountain Lion.

"Yes, the animals are fenced," replied Buzzard. "The animals are securely fenced with strong heavy mesquite posts and thorny branches spread over the fence," explained Buzzard.

"Now who dared to do such a mean thing? Buzzard, why didn't you open the gate and free the animals?" growled Coyote.

"Coyote, if you will hold your tongue I'll tell you all I've seen and heard," said Buzzard in his usual calm voice.

"It was while I rested on top of a butte, tired and very hungry, that I looked down upon the valley. I saw a dim outline of a corral. Then I saw a group of men open the corral gate, and a deer was led out and butchered just outside the corral. I flew down and walked over to see for myself. I overheard them speak about old man Mist. When I arrived, Mirage gave me a piece of meat to broil over the campfire. But I sat on a boulder nearby and pretended to take a nap. When they had finished their work, Mirage told the braves that Mist was waiting for the venison. Then they took all the meat and left for the village. Mist is the man who fenced in all the animals."

The Great Hunters stared at one another, too astonished to speak. Little Bobcat cried out, "At last old man Mist has us in his power!"

"Oh no! Not yet. We'll see who has power," snarled Coyote, ruffling his fur and showing his sharp teeth. "Let me go to the corral," begged Coyote. "I'll break down the gate and free the animals. We'll show old man Mist we five brothers cannot be starved."

"Coyote, be patient," scolded Mountain Lion in his deep voice. "We have been without food too long and we're too weak to give Mist a battle. We must have more food to give us strength before we strike back at our enemy."

"Then let me go, if only to get food," begged Coyote.

"Please give brother Coyote a chance to get food for us," coaxed little Bobcat.

"It's my turn to go," cried Raven. 'Like Buzzard I can fly to the corral and bring food sooner than Coyote, who is too slow."

"Raven, stop your boasting. You know that to fly is not everything," shouted Coyote, glaring at Raven. "You could not bring back enough food for all of us," he added.

"Then go! But don't you spoil everything with your foolishness," scolded Raven.

The brothers all agreed with Raven and warned Coyote not to do anything foolish. Coyote meekly promised to act with caution and wisdom.

"I'll go to bed now so I can get an early start," said Coyote.

True to his word, Coyote arose very early. In fact it was only a little after midnight when he started on his trip to get food for his hungry brothers. He went straight to the butte where Buzzard had directed him. Coyote sat on the butte a long time, but he saw nothing stirring. He was getting very impatient when suddenly he saw a group of braves approaching the corral.

"I should have been at the corral before the braves. But how was I to know that the dim outline down there was a corral." Coyote ran down the rugged slope of the butte.

"Every minute is precious," his thoughts ran. "My brothers need food badly. It is up to me to free the animals. Old man Mist is not going to starve us."

When Mirage looked up from his work, he saw Coyote running towards the corral. He knew Coyote and his crafty ways, but he felt that he must not reveal Coyote's name. The braves had often heard their parents tell of Coyote's crafty ways but had never seen him, so Mirage felt the wicked plan of Mist was safe.

"Another visitor is coming to our camp," he said. "I want every brave to be on guard for his tricks. He looks as if he is not to be trusted," warned Mirage, looking worried.

As soon as Coyote arrived, Mirage gave him a piece of meat to keep him busy, just as he had done with Buzzard.

"This venison is very good when you broil it over the live coals," suggested Mirage, pointing to the campfire. Coyote roughly grabbed the meat from Mirage and hungrily gobbled it up. Then he haughtily walked up to the corral and examined the gate.

"Get away from the corral," ordered Mirage, trying not to show his uneasiness.

"I only want to see the grandmother deer's eyes. Her antlers are so rusty! She must be so very, very old," said Coyote.

When Mirage turned his back for a fleeting moment Coyote hurriedly unfastened the latch and the restless animals ran out pell mell, nearly trampling down Mirage.

"See! What did I tell you?" angrily shouted Mirage to the astonished braves. "We must catch Coyote or else Mist will be very angry."

"Hi ya! Hi ya!" yelled the braves, waving their arms.

"Stop your yelling and catch Coyote," commanded Mirage. "Your yelling is frightening the animals and they're running further away."

"Coyote! Now we see. Coyote is one of the five

brothers. You and Mist are fighting the Great Hunters," said the Indian leader.

"We will not help you, Mirage, because the Great Hunters are our good friends," said another brave. The braves took all the meat they had prepared and returned to their homes in the village.

Mirage was left alone, and had to chase Coyote by himself. Coyote was far ahead, running in the opposite direction from home. He was aware of the danger he could bring to his starving brothers and he had to make a quick decision what to do. So he ran faster in the wrong direction. But no matter how fast Coyote ran he could not hide from angry Mist, who had seen everything from his mountain-top home.

"I'll help Mirage capture Coyote. He cannot go far," stormed Mist, covering the land with a heavy blanket of mist.

"The fame of the Great Hunters is lost already," said Mist with a wicked grin on his round face.

But Coyote blindly ran full speed ahead through the heavy fog. Mirage was losing ground, for he could not see Coyote in the heavy fog.

When Mist saw Coyote getting farther away from Mirage, he roared with all his might, "River, River, please help me catch Coyote."

River obeyed and ran swiftly across Coyote's way. Now, Coyote had never learned to swim, but he bravely jumped into the water. The swift current pushed him downstream, but as luck would have it, Coyote safely paddled across to the other side, took to his heels, and ran on faster than ever.

"Quicksand! Quicksand! Please help me catch Coyote," shouted Mist. Quicksand flung himself in the path of Coyote. But tired as he was, Coyote crawled forward on all fours, rolled his body over the layer of quicksand, and freed himself.

"Grab him, Quicksand, and don't let him go!" yelled angry Mist. "Is Coyote a better man than you?" taunted Mist when he saw Coyote getting away from Quicksand, too.

"I'll call Cholla Cactus. She'll show them how to catch Coyote," said Mist. "A woman usually does everything right."

"Cholla! Cholla! Please help me capture Coyote," cried Mist.

"I'll do my very best," softly answered Cholla Cactus, running and spreading her sharp thorns in the path of Coyote.

"A-na! A-na!" yelled poor Coyote in pain, hobbling across the thorn-covered ground. The sharp needles pierced Coyote's tired feet. Such hardships would have discouraged anyone else, but not Coyote. Besides, he was doing it for his brothers back home. Coyote again worked his way out of his trouble.

The sun setting behind the western hills told Coyote he was now far away from home. "At least my brothers are safe, and can have plenty to eat again," thought Coyote, pulling out the last thorn with his sharp teeth. At that moment Mirage came upon him.

"There you are, you scoundrel! I'll make sure you will not get away," said Mirage, reaching out his hands to catch Coyote by his bushy tail. Coyote wiggled and twisted his tail and broke away just as old man Mist arrived. Though Coyote was ready to drop, he ran on towards the setting sun with Mirage and Mist at his heels.

Suddenly Coyote saw a big body of water before him.

"I have no time to be afraid of the water. Indeed, my very life is in danger and who knows, the water may save me," reasoned Coyote as he jumped into the water to escape the clutches of his enemies, Mirage and Mist.

When Mirage saw Coyote leap into the ocean, he grinned, "My friend Mist, don't worry. Your troubles are over, for Coyote is drowned. That is certain."

"I will be certain of his drowning after four days have passed," thundered Mist, blowing up more fog.

They camped on the beach four days and four nights, Each day they looked for Coyote's body to be washed ashore. After four days had passed Mist was satisfied. "Well, I have won! The people of the village will appoint me their Chief. Mirage, my good friend, let us return to our village."

When the enemy was out of sight Coyote came ashore. He was a skinny, wet, and ragged-looking fellow!

"Ah, how good it is to be alive. Ha! Mist helped me without knowing it. His fog hid the tip of my nose when I held it above the water for air," said Coyote, stretching himself on the sandy shore. Coyote was very hungry and his empty stomach made such growling noises that he found it hard to rest. So he hobbled along the beach to look for food. Suddenly he heard someone singing. The singing came from a little piece of driftwood.

"Are my eyes and ears playing tricks on me?" he cried, turning over the piece of driftwood with one of his toes. To his great surprise it crawled into the ocean.

"A little snake! I could have had a good meal," cried Coyote. He walked on, and again he heard someone singing. Looking around, Coyote discovered a little round ball of mud. "How can this little ball of mud sing so loud?" said Coyote, turning it over and over to see if it had a mouth. Suddenly the ball of mud hopped into the ocean.

"A little frog!" wailed the hungry Coyote. "I could have had a good meal by now."

The many hardships Coyote had encountered caused his tired mind to forget who he was. And worst of all, he could not remember where he lived. All he could think of was food — food to quiet the growling noise in his stomach.

In the meantime his brothers were having plenty to eat, for the mesquite forests and plains were again alive with animals. But the hearts of the Great Hunters were very heavy because their brother Coyote had not returned.

"We know brother Coyote is the person who made it possible for us to have enough food to eat again. He faced all the danger alone and, who knows, he may even have lost his life," cried Mountain Lion, looking down his nose — a habit of his when deeply troubled.

"Give him time to come home," advised Buzzard, flapping his wings.

"He has had time to come home," sobbed Mountain Lion, giving way to his feelings and unashamedly wiping his teary eyes. "If he could find his way home he'd be with us now. We must find a way to bring brother Coyote home."

In the evening, under the guidance of Mountain Lion, the brothers filled a deer's intestines with fat and broiled it in the open firepit. When it was tender, little Bobcat took a sharp stick and with it punched holes in the cooked intestines. The appetizing odor of broiled fat drifted all over the land. Just as the Great Hunters desired, the odor reached their brother Coyote, who was searching for food by the seashore.

Sniff, sniff, sniff. Poor hungry Coyote never could resist the delicious odor of cooked fat, and at once he ran, sniffing the scent which led him straight home.

His brothers rejoiced to see Coyote and welcomed him with cries of joy. Little Bobcat could not hold back his happiness. He chanted and danced the victory song.

Mountain Lion took out his tom-tom and with a boom! boom! boom! kept time with Bobcat's chant. The chanting and beating of the tom-tom broke the evening stillness.

The people of the village heard and came in throngs to dance the victory dance. Coyote, by now fed and rested, joined in the merriment.

Later, Coyote was asked by the people, "How could you have been so brave?"

"Ha! that's nothing. Anyone can face danger to protect his loved ones," answered Coyote happily.

Coyote Retrieves His Brother's Scalp

AFTER COYOTE'S WARM WELCOME by his brothers and the people of the village, the Great Hunters enjoyed peace and happiness for only a short time.

Coyote was a lover of fun and excitement. But sometimes his foolishness caused pain, and brought shame to those whom he loved. So it was that Coyote innocently brought grief to his brothers.

"Ha! my brothers, your bows and arrows have not been kept in good condition," Coyote remarked one day. "Look at the strings, just about to break." Coyote ruffled his fur to show his disgust. He jerked off the strings and with fresh sinew restrung the bows. "Now I'll go out and find straight arrow-weeds for your new arrows. I know just the place."

Coyote started at once to find straight arrow-weeds.

On the way he saw Mother Bear gathering seeds from the salt bushes that grew near the hills.

"Ha! Mother Bear, why are you working so hard?"

"I have to work hard to feed my hungry children," answered Mother Bear. "Father Bear is so greedy. He eats all the meat and leaves only the bones for the children to lick."

"Come home with me. My brothers will give you some venison to take to your children."

"But Father Bear will be angry if I stay away from home too long."

"If you go with me now, you'll be home before Father Bear returns. You'll have venison to eat tonight," coaxed Coyote. It was such a tempting offer that Mother Bear could not resist. Besides, the children were tired of parched seeds. Venison would taste so good!

Mother Bear threw her basket on the ground and went with Coyote. It was dusk when they reached the home of the Great Hunters.

"My brothers, I've invited Mother Bear to come with me and have some good food to eat. We'll also give her some venison to take to her children," ordered Coyote. The brothers did as Coyote ordered. Food was given to Mother Bear who sat right down on the ground and enjoyed the venison.

Mountain Lion quietly took Coyote aside and scolded him.

"It is very wrong to bring Mother Bear here. You know Father Bear is a jealous fellow. He'll come and cause trouble."

"Aw! what's the harm? Her children are hungry for meat, and no doubt Father Bear is too," retorted Coyote.

In the meantime Father Bear had run out of patience with his crying children. "You wait here. I'll go find

Mother Bear," said Father Bear. He went straight to the salt-bush patch and found Mother Bear's basket lying in the bushes.

"Your children are crying," Father Bear shouted. There was no answer. Burning with rage, Father Bear looked of her tracks. He found the tracks of Mother Bear. Also the tracks of Coyote. Father Bear followed the tracks, which led him to the home of the Great Hunters.

"Mother Bear, your children are crying," thundered Father Bear. "Come; we must go home."

The brothers heard and cautioned each other not to awaken Coyote, who was asleep.

"Are you coming or not?" said Father Bear impatiently.

The noise awakened Coyote.

"What kind of talk is that? Give me my warclub. I'll have him know he can't talk in that manner around here."

"Coyote, be careful with your own tongue," warned Mountain Lion. But Coyote seized his warclub and ran out of the house to fight the Bear.

The Bear was very strong. He struck one blow, and poor Coyote fell dead on the hard ground.

One by one, Mountain Lion, Buzzard, and Raven went forth to avenge their brother's death. But these Great Hunters had been in a state of starvation so long that their strength was unequal to that of their foe and they also were killed.

Little Bobcat knew his strength would be useless, so he did not attempt to fight. He decided to try his magic on Father Bear.

After the battle was over Father Bear went into the *olas-ki* (round house) to look for Mother Bear. But during the fight, Mother Bear had silently gone home to feed her hungry children. In his search he found a smooth round stone above one of the rafters.

"What's this odd-looking little stone with black fearless eyes? It looks like a potter's stone." Bear scratched at the eyes, but the stone was so hard and slippery some of his claws broke off. Every time he scratched at the little stone more claws would break. When all his claws were broken, the stone turned back into the fierce Bobcat, who jumped on Bear's neck and chewed at his throat until he killed him.

Little Bobcat took a dipper of warm water and sang his song.

"Vom pom shu Maka."

He sprinkled the water on Coyote.

"Shah! I must have slept a long time," exclaimed Coyote, yawning and stretching his limbs.

"Asleep, nothing. You were killed by Father Bear," answered Bobcat. Resuming his singing, he sprinkled water also on Buzzard, Raven, and Mountain Lion.

When they were all revived, a council was held to decide how to celebrate their victory.

"A feast and dance is always our custom," said little Bobcat.

"Bobcat is right. I'll do the inviting," answered Coyote.

"Coyote, you may go, but don't do anything foolish. Sometimes I wonder if you have any sense!" warned Mountain Lion.

"Don't worry, Brother Mountain Lion," promised Coyote, and he ran to the village to invite the people there to come to a feast and dance.

Alas, Coyote, also went on to the Bear's village and invited the people there, too, thinking they were of his own clan.

The next day was a busy day for the Great Hunters. Food was cooked; the dance ground was swept very clean with arrow-weed brooms. Everything was ready for the merrymaking time. If the Great Hunters had known of their brother Coyote's mistake, they would have given up their victory dance.

Night had fallen when the people arrived wearing costumes. The Great Hunters were too busy with last-minute details to notice who their guests were.

The singers with gourd rattles sat in the middle of the dirt dance floor, and the celebration began. Everyone was having a merry time. Coyote ran into the house and came out dancing, holding something over his head. When he came near, the singing and dancing stopped. The people were shocked at what they saw. Coyote's brothers mumbled to one another. "Coyote is up to one of his tricks again. What is that he holds over his head?"

The Bear people cried, "Our brother's paws! We're not going to celebrate our own brother's death!" The Bear's clan pounced on Mountain Lion, scalped him alive and departed for their village, taking the scalp with them.

Buzzard angrily turned on Coyote, twisting his bushy tail. "Coyote, you idiot! When will you ever have some sense? Our brother Mountain Lion is in agony and filled with shame."

"Aw! I can fix it. Just you wait and see." Without another word Coyote chased after the enemy.

On the way he overtook a wrinkled little woman bent with old age.

"Where have you been, my friend?" gently asked Coyote.

"I've been to a dance. A rascal came to our village and invited our clan to their victory dance. During the dance the same old rascal came out dancing with our own brother Bear's paws. Our warriors scalped Mountain Lion and ran home. I'm old, so I'm tottering behind."

"I see," said Coyote. "Tell me, old woman, do you know your clan's victory song?"

'Of course I know our victory song," proudly answered the little old woman.

"Will you teach me the song?"

The old woman sang in her little squeaky voice, "'*Thaw van Yal lee.*"

"You sing so sweetly," encouraged Coyote. His scheme to get brother Mountain Lion's scalp was working.

Coyote sang the victory song with the old woman until he learned it.

"What's that rag you're carrying under your arm?"

"It's my *toon-ga* [costume]. I always wear it at ceremonials."

"My scheme is now complete," Coyote thought.

"May I carry the costume for you?" Coyote asked eagerly.

She gave him the *toon-ga*, and Coyote said, "Sorry, little old woman, but I'll have to hurry on. I want to help your people sing the victory song."

When Coyote reached the camp he quickly put on the costume, so that he looked just like the little old woman. "Now, to disguise my voice," and in a squeaky voice he sang the Bear Clan's victory song.

The people heard and shouted, "Give the scalp to the little old woman so that she can dance with it."

Coyote sang louder than ever imitating the old woman's squeaky voice. When Coyote received Mountain Lion's scalp he danced backward, then turned and ran for home as fast as he could. The Bear people were too tired to follow or even to ask why the little old woman ran away with the scalp.

When Coyote returned with his brother's scalp, Buzzard and Raven made fun of him.

"You can't put the scalp back on!" said Buzzard.

"The blood is dried up. Only a medicine man can fix it," said Raven.

"I'll show you." Coyote broke a piece of flintstone and with it rubbed his leg so hard it caused his blood to ooze. out. Then he rubbed the blood on Mountain Lion's head. He then took a giant cactus thorn for a needle, and with a string of sinew he sewed the scalp back on Mountain Lion's head.

"Brother, how do you feel now?" gently asked Coyote.

"I feel better already," answered Mountain Lion, and happy tears fell streaming down his face.

"Brother Mountain Lion, you are still a very handsome fellow. I hope Mother Bear will pay us another visit," teased Coyote, his eyes twinkling mischievously.

~

And this, the Pimas tell their children, is why there is a ring mark on a mountain lion's head. Next time you see a mountain lion, look for this mark.

Coyote's Trip to the Land Above

IN THE EVENINGS the birds and the animals of the desert gather around the campfire to discuss their travels and strange adventures.

One evening, Coyote, a curious and fun-loving fellow, attended the meeting. He was bursting with excitement and curiosity, for this night Buzzard was going to tell about his trip to the Land Above. And Buzzard, dignified personage of the Bird Clan, had promised to take Coyote along on his next trip.

As soon as Buzzard arrived, Coyote ran up to him and asked, "Brother Buzzard, I'm so eager to see the Land Above. Can't you take me now?"

Buzzard frowned at Coyote. "What is the reason for your eagerness?" he asked suspiciously. But he did not wait for Coyote's answer. He settled himself cozily with the rest of the Bird Clan around the blazing fire, and after everyone else had told his story, Buzzard began in a slow but clear voice to tell of his unbelievable trip to the Land Above.

"In my travels around this earth I've seen many interesting sights," Buzzard began.

"Why doesn't he come right to the point, and tell about the Land Above?" Coyote mumbled impatiently under his breath.

Buzzard paid no attention to this rudeness, but went on with his story. "However, the hills, valleys, and trees on earth were always the same. And I yearned for new adventures. One day when I was especially restless, I casually looked up to the sky and a tiny speck of cloud attracted my eyes. How thrilling it would be to feel about me the soft fleecy clouds and to enjoy the cool vapors far above earth!"

Coyote could not restrain himself. He blurted out, "Brother Buzzard, please come to the point. Stop all this nonsense about fleecy clouds and vapors. What about the Land Above?"

But dignified Buzzard pretended not to hear Coyote's interruption, and continued. "I flew towards the cloud, and soon flapped my wings in its soft folds. It was invigorating, like a dip in the blue water. I had the urge now to soar farther upwards."

"Now, that's more like it!" Coyote's sharp, pointed ears stood up as he leaned forward so as to hear Buzzard's every word.

"Up and up I traveled, until suddenly I noticed an entrance in the sky, like the entrance to a cave. And inside the entrance were signs of nature — tufts of green grass, shrubbery, and trees. I stopped and rested under one of the trees. 'I have found another world,' I thought.

And then a dim familiar noise like a tom-tom aroused me, and I set out to find where the noise came from. To my amazement, I found a large crowd of people singing and dancing to the beat of the tom-tom. I couldn't understand their language but the people were very friendly. And just like the people on earth! A game of chance was even in progress at one end of the gathering place!"

"Ho! Ho!" whispered Coyote, nudging little Bobcat, who sat next to him. "I can hardly wait to get in that game of *ginse*. I'll win up there — *they* don't know my tricks!"

Buzzard went right on with his story. "But suddenly a strange feeling came over me. What if these people should keep me a prisoner by closing the opening in the sky? I couldn't wait to get back to the entrance. The people were too busy dancing and playing games to notice that I had left, and when I found the entrance still open I was so relieved I returned home at once."

Buzzard gave a sigh of relief as he looked at his solemn-faced listeners. The bright campfire glow revealed their awe-stricken faces. They would not have believed the story if anyone less truthful than Buzzard had told it.

Their thoughts were interruped by Coyote's loud, gruff voice. "Brother Buzzard, will you take me to the Land Above tomorrow? I must see that place," pleaded Coyote. "They do not know me up there," he added slyly. Coyote wiggled his ears and long, bushy tail as he waited for Buzzard's reply.

Because of Coyote's eagerness, Buzzard hesitated to grant the mischievous Coyote's wish. But Coyote looked so pitiful with his pleading eyes that Buzzard didn't have the heart to deny him.

"Brother Coyote, I shall take you to the Land Above on one condition. You must promise to obey my orders.

Sometimes you are very foolish and do not use good judgment." To get his wish Coyote meekly promised to obey.

"Meet me here early tomorrow morning then," Buzzard said. "And now run home and get a good night's rest."

The next morning before sunrise Coyote was at the meeting place. He was a happy fellow! He sang and danced around the dead ashes of the fire that had burned so brightly last night. He even shrugged his shoulders and practiced all the motions of playing *ginse*. When Buzzard arrived and saw what Coyote was doing, he shook his small head with disapproval.

"You can't win the game of chance any more often up there than you can here," Buzzard said sagely. "The people will soon get wise to your tricks." Then Buzzard instructed Coyote to get on his back and close his eyes. "Do not open your eyes until we reach our destination," Buzzard ordered. "If you do as I say we will be safe on our trip. If not . . . who knows?"

"I'll do what you say," Coyote promised again.

Now they were ready, and Buzzard sang to the Wind God. In a deep voice he sang, "Wind God . . . Wind God . . . come and ease my burden on this trip to the Land Above."

The Wind God heard Buzzard's plea and came just as Buzzard spread his wings to rise slowly from the ground. Coyote felt Wind ruffling his shaggy fur. Higher and higher Buzzard flew with Coyote on his back, the Wind God softly pushing them on.

"I wonder what the Land Below looks like from here?" Coyote thought, and he was tempted to open one eye. But he remembered his promise just in time.

After what seemed an eternity they reached the entrance to the Land Above. Buzzard alighted near one of the trees. "You may open your eyes now," Buzzard said to Coyote. "And notice the place, notice the landmarks well. You must meet me here early tomorrow morning for our homeward trip. Do not fail to be here."

"I'll be here," Coyote promised. "You treat me like a child," he added growling. "I'll be here very early." And off he ran.

Buzzard shouted more good advice after him, but Coyote was already out of sight and did not hear a word.

When Coyote reached the gathering place Buzzard had told him about, his eyes almost popped out of their sockets. The people stared back with amusement at their visitor's strange appearance. But soon Coyote joined in the merriment and was too busy to care what the people said about him. The people took Coyote around to all their amusements, and before long he had managed to get in a game of chance. He used all his cunning tricks, and still he won only once! These people were wise to tricks like his. He even danced and tried to sing their songs. Coyote made everyone laugh with his gruff voice and his long, bushy tail swinging and brushing against their legs. Even if he could not win at *ginse* he was having a wonderful time!

He was having such a wonderful time, in fact, that he did not go to bed until very late. Then he looked for a place to rest his weary body, yawned, and curled up under a large bush where he slept soundly until late the next day. Not once did he remember Buzzard's instructions.

When he awoke, he sat up wondering, "Where am I?" And then Buzzard's instructions flashed across his mind. He jumped up and ran to the entrance. Buzzard had already departed for the land below!

"I don't want to stay up here any longer!" wailed

Coyote. "I want to be with my own clan. Perhaps the Wind God will help me back to earth if I sing for help." But the Wind God, too, had departed for the land below.

Coyote walked a little way from the entrance and, with tears rolling down his long face, he sang:

"Va se va se loo-ooo
O va se va se loo kum
O va se va se loo
O va se va see loo."

When his song ended, Coyote ran towards the entrance, intending to jump — only to lose courage and stop. Because Coyote had been so foolish and had not obeyed Buzzard's orders, the only way he could get home was to jump. After the fourth attempt, Coyote closed his eyes tightly and jumped into space.

Down, down he fell. And since the earth was so far below, poor Coyote died from cold and hunger on the way down. All that remained of Coyote were his falling bones.

In the meantime Buzzard flew back to the Land Above. "By now," he thought, "Coyote will have learned his lesson."

Buzzard searched everywhere, but Coyote was not to be found. Buzzard's deep-set eyes were troubled, for he had loved Coyote in spite of his mischievous ways. Closely examining the ground near the entrance, Buzzard found Coyote's tracks. "Just what I thought!" he cried. "He must have tried several times to jump. The grass is all trampled like the ground of a medicine man's trodden path." Sadly Buzzard abandoned his search and returned home.

One evening when the birds and animals were gathered around their campfire they spoke of Coyote. Mountain

Lion said, "Many a moon has passed and our brother Coyote is still sadly missed."

While they were discussing their lost brother a strange noise was heard just above their heads. And, before anyone could look up, a heap of old gray bones fell with a thud at their feet. The other animals were frightened and dumb-founded, but Buzzard recovered his voice and with a tremble said, "I know these bones in our midst are Coyote's. He once told me that should he precede me to the Happy Hunting Grounds I must take care of his burial."

Buzzard then arose and with the help of the other birds and animals gathered up every bone, and buried them in the soft ground. Then the animals and birds sadly returned to their homes, unaware of a happier surprise that was in store for them.

Before sunrise next morning familiar cries were heard in the distance. Coyote's cries! From Brother Coyote's bones the Great Spirit had made many little coyotes to carry on Coyote's curious and fun-loving nature.

And thereafter the howls of the coyotes could be heard in the land at sunrise and at sunset, to proclaim to the land that Brother Coyote was not lost after all.

Why Coyote's Coat Is the Color of Sand

COYOTE HAD OFTEN WONDERED why his friends stared at him with amused eyes. One bright day he found the answer. He discovered his shabby grey coat in the mirror of the clear blue water of the river.

"So that is how I look, faded and shaggy, like an old man," Coyote wailed as he walked beside the blue river.

He remembered then his little friend Bluebird, who had once told him of a magic lake in which he bathed to restore his old faded feathers to their original beautiful blue.

"Perhaps Bluebird can help me," cried Coyote.

The next day Coyote called on Bluebird in the woods.

"I need your help, my friend," said Coyote, sadly looking at his shabby coat. "My coat is so faded! Do you think you could help me to get a blue coat like yours?"

"It will be very simple," answered Bluebird, glancing at Coyote with pity. "Come with me to my magic lake. I need to renew my coat too."

They started at once for the magic lake, which was at the edge of a dense forest.

On their journey Bluebird gave Coyote some advice.

"There are some rules to follow, Coyote, if you want to use the magic lake. After your coat is changed to a beautiful blue color you must not look at your coat until four days have passed."

"I will do anything you say," promised Coyote eagerly.

"And you must not look at your shadow, either, until four days have passed," added Bluebird. "If you do not follow these rules your coat will turn back to the same faded color."

Coyote didn't like the rules. He didn't see how he could wait four days to see himself in a beautiful coat. But what else could he do? He needed a new coat, so he agreed to do everything his little friend said.

When they arrived at the lake, Blue Bird stood on the shore and shrilly sang his magic song.

"Clear blue water,
change my faded hue
into a pretty blue."

After each singing, Bluebird jumped into the lake. He went through the same process four times. Each dip made his faded coat turn a brighter blue. Coyote's eyes twinkled merrily.

"I'll be the most handsome fellow in the world," he whispered, happily waiting his turn to have his coat changed. He sang along with Bluebird to learn the magic words and before long was singing the whole song at the top of his voice.

When Bluebird came ashore the fourth time he had a beautiful blue coat.

"Coyote, you have learned all the things you should do to obtain your wish. Remember my warning, and your coat will be beautiful too." Bluebird flew away and left Coyote alone by the lake. The time had come.

Coyote imitated his friend, singing and jumping into the magic lake in quick succession. After the fourth dip, he came ashore a new creature. How eager he was to get back to the village to show his friends his bright shiny new coat!

As he walked along the sandy trail that led to the village, Coyote was full of high spirits.

"I'll be envied by the whole tribe. Now the people will not make me a laughingstock," Coyote said proudly.

But alas! Coyote forgot Bluebird's second rule. He glanced slyly at his shadow. At that moment his foot bumped on a mesquite stump in the middle of the path, and he fell headlong in the sand. Coyote hurriedly jumped up and shook his body this way and that way, but without any result. The sand had covered his wet coat and would not come off.

He ran back to the magic lake and again went through the complete process of singing and dipping. But it was hopeless. Coyote finally gave up and sadly went home.

～

And that is why Coyote's coat today is the color of sand.

Turtle Feeds His Children

TURTLE COULD NOT BEAR to hear his children crying for food. "I must find food for the children," said Turtle.

He went to the hills to hunt for antelope. The sun passed quickly overhead, and still Turtle had not found any food.

Tired from crawling over a large area of rough country, he stopped under a pine tree to rest. Suddenly he noticed all around him the tracks of antelopes. He was resting on the antelope trail, and hadn't realized it.

"I'll lie here on their trail and wait for them," said the happy Turtle.

Before long Turtle heard the soft steps of antelopes coming down the trail. He had a plan and decided to use it — anything to get food for the children.

Turtle sang loud and clear, "Antelopes with shiny, skinny limbs. With large twitching mouths."

"I am not letting anyone as low and common as Turtle poke fun at us," said the first antelope. "Let's crush him to death!" said the second antelope.

The first antelope ran up and stamped on Turtle. But Turtle's back was so very hard and slippery, that the antelope fell, breaking his neck. The second antelope, seeing what happened, also ran forward and stamped on Turtle with all his might. And he also fell and broke his neck.

Turtle was indeed a proud and happy fellow! He broke down rocks from a big boulder to use as sharp tools with which to skin the dead antelopes.

Coyote, who has a habit of arriving just at the right time, heard Turtle singing.

"Why are you so very happy, my brother Turtle?" Coyote asked.

"I have killed two antelope," answered Turtle very proudly.

"May I help you?" asked sly old Coyote.

They went to work cutting the antelope meat. Then, when Turtle was not looking, Coyote took his lariat, threw the noose around Turtle's neck and fastened the rope end around a branch. Though Turtle wiggled and pleaded to be let down, Coyote left him dangling from a tree. Coyote picked out the choicest cuts of meat and departed for home.

When Coyote reached his home he shouted, "Children, I've killed some antelope and here's the meat."

The children took big bites from the meat and began to cry.

"What is the matter now?" Coyote asked impatiently.

"The meat is full of ants and scorpions," cried the children.

"Nonsense!" said Coyote and took a bite of the meat.

"A-na! A-na! My mouth is burning," cried Coyote, running in circles, for the pain was great.

"Turtle is punishing me. I forgot he has magic power," wailed Coyote.

"But I'll get even with Turtle."

Coyote ran back to the tree where he had tied Turtle. But Turtle was not there. Coyote followed Turtle's tracks to a little brook. He saw Turtle lying on the bottom of the brook, for the water was very clear.

"Birds and animals of the woods! Come and drink up this water," ordered sly old Coyote.

When the water was low enough for Coyote to see Turtle's back above the water, he shouted to the birds and animals, "Stop drinking."

Coyote jumped in the water and was about to dig his sharp teeth into poor little Turtle when the water rose and Coyote was drowned.

Turtle crawled out of the brook and returned to the place where he had butchered the antelopes. He happily took the rest of the meat home and fed his hungry children.

The Quail Clan Punishes Coyote

IT WAS A BRIGHT, WARM DAY when the Quail Clan held a meeting to find a way to stop Coyote from making life unbearable for them.

"What I can't bear is when Coyote chases us up a tree and we cannot come down to eat and drink water," said a large quail.

"We must punish Coyote. It is the only way to stop him from his pranks," said the Chief. "We will need four willing quail to play the joke on Coyote."

Four members of the Quail Clan agreed to help in the plan.

"First we'll need some of your feathers." Several quail came forward with their plucked feathers. "Now two of you get sticks and push that dry cholla pod over here," commanded the Chief.

When the thorny piece of cactus was in place, the Chief covered it with the soft feathers. The quail laughed at the disguised cactus. It looked so much like a live quail.

Now they pushed the feathered cholla down a hole in the ground made by a badger.

"You four volunteers stand near the hole and get ready to play your joke on Coyote. The rest may sit in the tree close by and watch him get his punishment," directed the Chief.

Before long the quail saw Coyote running with his nose close to the ground. He was sniffing at the quail tracks.

The four quail sang with all their might, "Coyote is a foolish fellow!"

"Who dares to make fun of me?" growled Coyote.

"We dare to make fun of you," answered the four quail.

"You little birds dare to make fun of me?" asked Coyote, not believing he had heard correctly.

"Yes, yes, yes," bravely answered the quail.

Coyote was so very angry he ran to grab the quail. But they were too quick and scurried into the badger hole where the cholla was hidden. Panting, and burning with anger, Coyote reached into the hole and grabbed a quail.

"Were you the one?" he asked.

"The next one," answered the first bird.

Coyote let him go. He reached into the hole again and brought out the second quail.

"Were you the one?" he asked.

"The next one," said the second quail.

The third and fourth quail answered likewise and were let go.

Finally Coyote reached into the hole for the fifth quail and asked, "Were you the one?"

There was no answer.

"Ah, now I have caught the culprit! You dare not answer because you are the one."

Coyote dug his sharp teeth into what he thought was a quail.

"*A-na, A-na,*" cried Coyote, with his mouth wide open. The sharp cholla needles were sticking all over his mouth.

Coyote learned his lesson. He never chased the quail birds again.

Little Frog Repays Coyote

COYOTE WAS WALKING in the meadow near the river when he heard his name called. "Who's using my name?" he growled. He stopped to listen. Again he heard his name, this time used in a chant. "I'm going to search until I find the chanter," he said to himself.

Coyote ran towards the place where the chanting was coming from. He could not see anyone. He stopped and listened. Again he heard singing. It seemed to come from a pile of dry cottonwood leaves. Coyote stood very still.

The chant started again. It *was* coming from the pile of dry leaves. Coyote grew very angry, for he was being ridiculed. This is the song he heard.

> *"Bonai Bonai Bonai!*
> Coyote! Coyote! Coyote!

Swal-mag au voo pwi!
With teary, smudgy eyes!
Si-kiljals au Chin-ni ka!
Serrated is his mouth!
Scoosth wa au by-he-ka!
Bushy is his tail!"

Ah Sheo oo! Coyote was ready to fight! He could
not stand being ridiculed in this fashion. Pushing aside
the dry leaves he discovered the singer. At first Coyote
could not believe his eyes. For under the leaves crouched
a tiny, green frog no bigger than one of his toes.

"So, you are the one who is making fun of me?"

"Yes," answered the little green frog. He was very
bold because he was a medicine man. He had magic power.

"*Sha!* I am going to have some fun," said Coyote,
bristling his coat.

"If you hurt me I'll drown you," answered the frog.

"I'm going to dig my teeth into your little fat body. But
first I'll just roll you around in my mouth."

"I'll cause a big flood to come and drown you," said
the frog.

Coyote did not know the little frog was a *makai* (medicine man). If he had, perhaps Coyote would have been
more careful. As it was, he snapped him up between his
jaws and rolled the little frog around, first to the right
cheek, then to the left. Alas! Coyote accidentally swal-
lowed the little green frog.

Soon the winds came, bringing the rain. The river
overran its banks. Coyote ran to the nearest willow tree
and climbed as high as he could go. "*Oose athaw Chive
ve* — tree will shiver," he cried. He sat in the tree a long,
long time. So long, in fact, that he was getting very
hungry.

Finally the river began slowly going down. Then Coyote saw two big birds with long legs passing by beneath him. On their heads they carried large, thick loaves of bread.

"My friends, please give me some of your bread. I'm so hungry. I'll die if you don't help me," pleaded Coyote. The long-legged birds looked up and saw Coyote perched in the tree.

"Come down from the tree. We'll give you some bread to eat."

"But is the water deep?"

"No, Coyote, it's not deep. See the sand," said the birds, tossing up some river sand with their feet. Of course, to them it was shallow because of their long legs.

But, although he was terribly hungry, Coyote was too afraid of the water to jump down from the tree.

Finally, one of the birds came under the willow tree where Coyote was perched. "Get on my back. I'll carry you across to dry land."

Coyote did as he was told. They had not gone far when naughty Coyote leaned forward to the bird's ear and whispered, *"Gu oose kai heoh kum* — You have stick legs."* It was not a nice thing to say, was it? Especially when the big bird was being so kind as to carry Coyote on his back.

"Say it again and I'll drown you," said the big bird. Coyote should have stopped, but no, he said it again, *"Gu oose kai heoh kum."*

The big bird, which today we call Heron, suddenly threw Coyote into the river. Coyote drowned.

Heron had helped the little green frog — the medicine man — repay Coyote.

Coyote's Vanity

LITTLE REDBIRD gracefully hopped back and forth on the branch of a willow tree. Winter was nearly over. It was time to change her faded red coat. "Spring will soon be here. I want my coat to be bright red," said Redbird, flitting back and forth singing a lively song.

> *"Chee chee paw nee*
> *Chee chee paw nee*
> *Chee gall lee*
> *Chee gall lee."*

Coyote, who was passing by, heard the little bird's song. As he listened, he watched Redbird plucking out her feathers.

"Redbird, why are you so happy this morning?" asked Coyote. "And why do you sing, *'Chee chee paw nee'?"*

"I need a bright new coat for Spring," answered Redbird.

"May I stay here and learn your song? I need a bright coat too," asked Coyote.

When pretty little Redbird's coat was changed to bright red, she flew away.

"Now it's my turn," said Coyote. He climbed on a low branch of the tree. Coyote had never climbed a tree before and was afraid to climb any higher. Proudly he straightened up his head. In a high-pitched voice he sang Redbird's song. *"Chee chee paw nee."*

Every now and then Coyote would stop and pull out his fur with his sharp teeth. At last he thought he saw a speck of red fuzz on his body. So he continued to trot back and forth on the willow branch singing and pulling out his fur.

The sun went down behind the big mountain. Coyote's voice was growing hoarse and weak. The night air was turning cold and Coyote shivered. Still he feebly sang for a bright new coat. Yes, just like Redbird's coat.

In the morning the people of the village found Coyote's bare body lying under the willow tree. Because Coyote wanted a pretty coat, his foolishness had cost him his life.

~

When a Pima child commits a foolish act, his parents warn him not to be foolish and vain like the *Bun* (Coyote).

Coyote Bun and the Turkey

IT WAS A BEAUTIFUL DAY in the village of Thawsin. The people were stirring about in preparation for their daily tasks.

In the village lived Coyote Bun and his wife, whom he teasingly called "Awks," or "old woman." All was not well with the Buns. They were continually quarreling because Coyote Bun was lazy and foolish, while Awks worked very hard grinding corn on her little *metate*.

This bright morning Coyote Bun's large yellow eyes twinkled merrily and he asked, "Awks Bun, how would you like to eat a nice fat turkey today?"

"I'd like to eat turkey meat for a change. I'm so tired of parched corn. But there is no use wishing. You were never a skilled hunter," said Awks Bun, giving a big sigh.

"Oh! Oh! I've started her nagging again," mumbled

Coyote Bun under his breath. He decided to be very careful not to arouse his wife's temper. "Antelope told me the turkeys are plentiful in the northern woods," cheerfully related Coyote Bun. "And I intend to have one."

When their frugal meal of corn broth was over, Coyote Bun took his crude stone ax and departed for the woods. "Awks, I'll be back with a big fat turkey. Keep your pot boiling," commanded Coyote Bun.

"I'll wait until I see the turkey," answered Awks Bun, shaking her head. She was thinking of the countless times Coyote Bun had uttered those words, only to return empty-handed.

Coyote Bun went directly to the place to which Antelope had directed him. He stopped and listened. "Do I hear someone singing?" he whispered. He perked up his sharp ears and listened intently. "Yes, I hear a number of voices," he said happily. Stealthily he tiptoed towards the thick bushes. His yellow eyes sparkled at what he saw through the bushes. His large mouth drooled, and he wiggled his long bushy tail. He was glad he had believed Antelope. A flock of turkeys was gathered around a pine tree. They were singing and pounding at the trunk of the tree.

Coyote Bun stepped out from his hiding place. He asked, very gently, so as not to frighten the turkeys, "My turkey brothers, may I ask just what you are doing?"

The astonished and frightened turkeys looked up from their work.

"We are chopping down this pine tree," answered the leader.

"May I help you, my turkey brothers?" asked sly old Coyote Bun, and went to work with his stone ax. Suddenly the tree fell, and a large heavy branch pinned Coyote Bun's long, bushy tail.

"Run for your lives," shouted the leader. "He's a sly old Coyote and does not really care to help us." The turkeys scampered in every direction.

Coyote wiggled and wiggled but without any luck. He shouted after the turkeys, "My turkey brothers, I have a message from the Chief. Please stop and I will tell you."

The turkeys reasoned, "It may be something very important. Let us stop and hear the message."

Coyote Bun wiggled and finally was free from the heavy branch. He jumped up quickly and raced after the turkeys, who saw he had no message for them and ran faster. "I must not disappoint Awks again," he moaned. Coyote Bun's wish to please Awks prodded him on faster than ever.

At last, just around the bend of the path, he saw the turkeys resting under a large pine tree.

"Ho! Ho! Here's my chance to grab a fat turkey," he thought.

When he arrived, panting and out of breath, Coyote Bun's eyes wandered over the turkeys. "I'll stand by the largest turkey to give you the Chief's message," said sly old Coyote Bun.

"Better watch Coyote Bun, he's a . . ." warned the leader. But that was as far as he got with the warning. Coyote Bun grabbed the largest turkey and laughed with joy while the other turkeys ran away to safety.

Then Coyote said to the turkey he had grabbed, "My turkey brother, I want you to go to my house in Thawsin. Tell my wife to chop off your head and cook you for dinner. Tell her to save me your head. I'm very fond of turkey head."

"I'll do just as you say," said the scared turkey, trying not to show his relief.

Coyote Bun turned his back on the largest turkey and

without another word chased after the rest of the turkeys, who were now all out of sight.

"He's certainly very foolish," reasoned the largest turkey. "But I'm glad he's foolish or I'd be in the Happy Hunting Grounds right now."

Turkey trudged along the dusty path, planning just what he would say to Coyote Bun's wife. "I hope she's just as foolish as her husband. I'll show them I can outsmart both of them," boasted the fat turkey.

The sun was nearly overhead when he reached the home of Coyote Bun. Awks Bun was grinding parched corn. She was startled to see a big fat turkey come before her and speak.

"Your husband Coyote Bun asked me to stop by and tell you he wants his best bearskin sandals cooked. He's been detained, but will be home when the sun is directly overhead. It is nearly that time now and I must be on my way," said the turkey, looking up at the sun.

Awks Bun was so astonished she said not a word. She stared at the turkey with her mouth wide open, letting the turkey get away from her too!

After the turkey was out of sight, Awks Bun remembered her husband's foolish instructions. "Well, I'll cook his best sandals to punish him," said Awks with the usual angry jerk of her head. She tossed the bearskin sandals into her earthen pot and added more wood to the fire.

Tired and hungry, Coyote Bun finally gave up the chase. He turned back towards home, his mouth watering at the happy prospect of a nice turkey dinner.

The sun was directly overhead when, dusty and hungry, he reached his home. "Awks, is the turkey ready to eat?" he called. "It smells good. I can hardly wait to dig my teeth into the turkey's head."

"Your bearskin sandals are nice and tender," answered his wife.

"What! My best sandals?" growled Coyote Bun. "What is the meaning of this?"

His wife told how a big turkey had stopped by and given her his foolish message.

"Now who's foolish?" Coyote Bun cried. "Why didn't you grab him and chop off his head? Now I must track him down again, and catch him." Without stopping to sit down to his meal, Coyote Bun fished one of his cooked sandals from the pot, taking big bites from it as he hurried to catch up with the turkey.

The turkey's tracks led to a little brook where a large willow tree branch leaned lazily over the water. Coyote Bun stood at the water's edge. Suddenly he saw the turkey in the water.

"There you are!" snarled the angry Coyote Bun. He shouted to Awks, "Bring your *metate*. I've found the turkey in the brook. I'll watch him well. He'll not get away this time."

Before long Awks Bun arrived, carrying her *metate* in her burden basket.

"Awks, strap the *metate* on my back," ordered Coyote Bun, giving her a long strip of young willow bark. "I'll get into the brook after the turkey, with the *metate* to hold me down. We'll have him for our dinner, just you wait and see." Awks did as she was told and strapped the heavy *metate* on her husband's back.

Coyote Bun jumped into the water, sank to the bottom, and was drowned while Awks stood helplessly by.

The creaking of a willow branch above her head caused Awks to look up. In the tree was the fat turkey, grinning down at her! Awks realized too late it was only the turkey's reflection in the water that her husband had seen. Now poor foolish Coyote Bun had drowned.

Awks quickly grabbed her burden-basket prop stick and angrily poked at the turkey. Whereupon the turkey flew down and ran away to the northern woods to tell how he had bested Coyote Bun.

Coyote Eats His Own Fat

ONE SUMMER DAY an old Quail and his little brother decided to take a stroll.

"We'll go to Crooked Mountain [Superstition Mountain]," said the oldest Quail, gazing towards the tall mountain standing so majestically in the desert land of the Red men.

The Quails started on their jaunt, not forgetting their friction sticks and their little round crystal magic stone.

"Too many wild beasts roaming on Crooked Mountain. We must be ready for them."

Before going very far they discovered Coyote fast asleep under a shady palo verde tree. "Sha! Here's the chance we've been waiting for. Coyote will not play his tricks on us any more," the oldest Quail remarked defiantly.

"But we're so little. Coyote will eat us up with one

gulp," warned the tiniest Quail, looking very frightened.

"Have you forgotten the magic powers given to us by Pi-Shava, the great medicine man of Vah-ki village?" answered the oldest Quail, looking at his little magic crystal stone.

"Pi-Shava warned us that four days must elapse before our magic powers can work," said the tiniest Quail.

"Stop your quivering, my little brother. The four days have already passed since this morning at sunrise."

The Quails quickly picked up two stones lying on the side of the trail. Then they started to put Coyote into a deep sleep by blowing puffs of tobacco smoke into the nostrils of their victim.

"This will teach you never to chase us up on the trees and deprive us of food and water."

"You said it, brother," agreed the tiniest Quail, blowing more smoke over Coyote to make certain their powers worked.

The sleepy Coyote yawned, relaxed and stretched out his limbs, thereby making himself an easy prey. The oldest Quail opened Coyote's stomach with a sharp flint and scooped out a large piece of fat. Then the tiniest Quail threw in the two stones to replace the fat. "We had better be on our way," said the tiniest Quail, who was still suspicious and afraid of Coyote. They knew Coyote was in a deep sleep unaware of the plot against him. The Quails resumed their walk toward Crooked Mountain.

When a distance of several miles was between them and the sleeping Coyote, they stopped to complete their trick on their helpless victim. The birds gathered some mesquite wood and started a fire by rubbing their friction sticks. Soon the flames danced very brightly and the odor of the burning mesquite wood was so very pleasant to inhale. The Quails waited until the flames died down and only the red glowing embers remained. Then they threw Coyote's fat on the hot embers to broil. They turned the fat over and over with a long saguaro-cactus pole until it was just right. The odor drifted all over the land of the red men.

Coyote at that moment was awakened from his slumber by a mother dove cheerfully twittering while feeding her young in the palo verde tree over head.

"Shah! I must have slept a long, long time," exclaimed Coyote. He jumped up from the ground and stretched his limbs this way and that way. "Aw! My stomach feels so empty," he wailed and gently rubbed it. "Hum-m-m! What is smelling so good?" Coyote immediately started to find out where the delicious odor was coming from. Of course Coyote did not know he was the victim of the little Quails he had abused many a time with his pranks. He also did not know the odor was from his own cooked fat.

When Coyote trotted along the rugged and narrow Indian foot trail, he heard strange knocking noises in his stomach and felt a sharp pain. Every time Coyote stopped running, the knocking sounds and the pain would also stop. "What's happened to me?" he wondered. "Is it because I'm so hungry?"

Coyote wanted food! Food! Food! So he ran as fast as his legs could carry him in spite of the pain and the knocking sounds in his stomach. He followed the tempting odor until he reached the fireplace by the side of the trail. He saw the Quails placing the roasted fat on a slab of rock to cool.

"Ummm, ummm! The roast is nice and brown. Looks good. I'm so hungry!" exclaimed Coyote to the Quails, and without waiting for a reply, Coyote roughly grabbed it from the slab of rock. He greedily ate the fat with one gulp. This was too funny and more than the Quails could bear. They made little giggling noises in their throats but they quickly covered their mouths to prevent the laughter from bursting forth. It was really just too much to see Coyote eating his own fat. The Quails turned their backs on Coyote in order to hide their grinning faces.

"What's the meaning of your giggling sounds?" snarled Coyote. "Why do you turn your backs on me?" he growled again, ruffling his shaggy coat and displaying his white, sharp fangs.

"Hold your temper, Coyote. We're delighted to share our food with you," answered the tiniest Quail, trying to keep from laughing.

"My little brother is right," agreed the oldest Quail.

"Well, my stomach is still very empty," said Coyote loudly smacking his lips. "I'll have to scrounge around for more food on Crooked Mountain." Then Coyote started in search of more food.

Just as soon as Coyote was out of sight the Quail began dancing around, laughing so very hard that tears streamed down their faces just like *vomat-juhk* — snake rain (steady, drizzling rain — slick and slippery like a snake). So happy were they because at last they had won by the help of the crystal magic stone given to them by Pi-Shava the medicine man.

"There is still one more thing we must do if our troubles are to be completely over," said the oldest Quail.

"What's that?" asked the tiniest Quail with aroused curiosity.

"We have to ridicule Coyote. He must be told about the trick we played on him while he was soundly sleeping under the palo verde tree," answered the oldest Quail.

"He'll be so ashamed that he'll not dare to play tricks on us," chimed in the tiniest Quail.

"Now you're talking like a man," said brother Quail. It was decided that the only way they could carry out their plan was to join in a chant so Coyote could hear it. They cleared their throats and chanted,

"Coyote Ate His Own Fat!
Coyote Ate His Own Fat!"

The gentle breeze carried the chant, and the sharp ears of Coyote caught every word. "Coyote ate his own fat!" "So that is why I've been so famished," reasoned Coyote. The knocking sounds now made sense. "The little Quails have tricked me. I'll run back and punish them."

Coyote arrived at the roasting place but the Quails were nowhere in sight. Only the dead ashes and slab of rock were there to remind Coyote of his unhappy experience.

The truth of the matter was that the Quails were hiding in the mesquite thicket anxiously waiting to see their victim's reaction to all the hardship he was encountering.

Coyote looked haggard for he knew he was defeated. Then the past bad treatment his little friends had received from him flashed before him. "I have been too hard on the Quails," Coyote said to himself. "Well, it is going to stop, and I am going to tell them now."

Coyote cleared his throat, "A-hem!" and shouted for the Quails to hear. "My little Quail friends, I have decided never to play tricks on you again."

Coyote and the Quails became very warm friends.

Legend of the Roadrunner

LONG AGO when the world was new, Thadai, the Road-runner, had beautiful, long plumage.

One day when the Indians returned from the hunt, they discovered their fire had died down; only the gray ashes remained. The Indians prevailed upon Roadrunner to run to Lightning-God, keeper of the Fire, and ask him for one of his fire-sticks.

Roadrunner, being a good fellow, agreed and started at once for the mountain home of Lightning-God. His strong legs helped him to "fold up the earth" (make good time); soon he reached his destination.

"What brings you here?" asked Lightning-God.

"The Indians badly need fire."

"No!" Lightning-God angrily retorted.

Roadrunner realized it was useless to ask again, so the

first chance he had, he snatched one of the fire-sticks from the blazing fire. Hastily placing it across his back and curling his tail over it, he scampered away. Lightning-God grabbed some flaming arrows and began shooting at Roadrunner. At the same moment Roadrunner saw an arroyo and scurried into it, escaping the arrows. But the beautiful plumes on his head were burnt off, leaving only a small tuft. His back was singed so that it became a brownish color, and his eyes turned red from the smoke he endured.

Roadrunner successfully brought the fire-stick to the Indians. When the squaws saw his tired red eyes and his short, stiff bushy head they loudly wailed, *"Shoik, Shoik, Shoik"* (Poor bird). Roadrunner was touched by their display of love and wailed,

"Poi, Poi, Poi."

Ever since then the Roadrunner has made his home in the chaparral. Whenever he finds a fat lizard he cheerfully chants, *"Thra, Thra, Thra!"* When the Indians hear his chant they smile gratefully remembering what Roadrunner did for them.

Beaver Tail and the Eagles

A SHORT DISTANCE from his adobe house, Beaver Tail alighted from his black pony, Thunder. The Indian boy's face was beaming with pride.

"I'm a man now," he though, proudly holding at arm's length his first bunch of quail. Beaver Tail was twelve when he began helping his father hunt the wild game for meat. But now he was thirteen, and he wanted to do more than just help his father.

Beaver Tail more than anything else longed to find some eagles, and all by himself. Finding an eagle's nest is considered quite an honor among the Pima youth of Arizona. Lately, Beaver Tail's gaze had often wandered towards distant Tall Red Mountain (Camelback Mountain).

"I wonder if there are eagles on that red mountain?"

Beaver Tail thought. "I'll ask Mother," and he quickened his steps into the house. His mother's face brightened with a warm welcome. She laid aside the basket she was weaving and looked up at her son. "Mother, do you know, are there eagles on Tall Red Mountain?" he asked, placing the quail on the crude table.

"Yes, son," his mother replied, "but don't go over there. It's a long, tiresome journey and the mountain is too steep for climbing. Remember what your father said about killing birds for sport. It's cruel." His mother picked up her basket and resumed her weaving.

"But, Mother, all I want to do is use the eagles for pets. I may give some of the eagle feathers to Hal Bee, the Medicine Man. He needs them in curing the sick."

"Hush, Beaver Tail!" scolded his mother, her eyes flashing with anger, "Don't ever help Hal Bee. He does not belong to our clan. We learned that Hal Bee brings sickness to our clan. That's the reason my sister, Squash Blossom, is still ailing." And the woman angrily poked her sharp awl into her basket to emphasize her just indignation.

Beaver Tail's father and mother had just been told about Hal Bee's false practice. They were rather strict with their only son, Beaver Tail. But in spite of what his mother said, the young boy's mind was definitely made up. He was going to climb Tall Red Mountain tomorrow.

The Indian boy haughtily stalked out of the house. He unsaddled his pony and placed an armful of fresh hay before him.

"Thunder, ol' boy! Eat all the hay. Tomorrow we will go to Tall Red Mountain to search for my favorite pets, *napawchick*, baby eagles," said Beaver Tail, gently stroking Thunder's black mane.

At break of day Beaver Tail stole quietly out of the

adobe house. He saddled his pony and rode away toward Tall Red Mountain. His bow and arrows were in his quiver, his shield was on the saddle's pommel, the little gourd vessel was full of fresh water and securely tied on back of the saddle.

It was many hours past his breakfast time when he reached a small creek. He unbridled his pony to let it drink the cool water and to nibble on the green grass growing at the water's edge while he hungrily ate a piece of the flour tortilla he had carried in one of his pockets.

After resting a while, Beaver Tail continued on his journey over the long stretch of desert. To break the monotony of the ride through cactus, sagebrush, and mesquite trees, Beaver Tail sang. The lad's young tenor voice broke into a song he had learned from Owl Ear, the storyteller, *"Thaw von ya-lee, Thaw von ya-lee."* Then he would imitate the little mourning dove's coo-coo! coo-coo! The sun beat down unmercifully but Beaver Tail's determination to find his pets on Tall Red Mountain did not weaken.

Beaver Tail arrived at the foot of the mountain at noon. He tied his horse under a large shady palo verde tree, and drank water from his gourd vessel. Now to ascend the high mountain. He looked up at the rugged slope. His mother was right, the mountain was risky; but Beaver Tail was going to climb it or die in the attempt.

He labored up, resting on every flat rock. "Whew! The sun is as hot as a branding iron," he moaned, wiping the perspiration from his face, his eyes smarting. He clutched wildly at bushes and thorny barrel cactus to avoid falling into the deep gorges yawning on every side of him. With hands bruised and blistered, he finally reached the top of Tall Red Mountain.

"Whee! I made it!" he exclaimed, slumping against

a big red boulder. If it had not been for his shining black hair, Beaver Tail would have been invisible. His complexion was so nearly the color of the red boulder behind him.

"So this is it," the lad muttered aloud, looking about at the mountain top. His father had told him about the mountain. His ancestors had named it centuries ago, and legends were told about it. Beaver Tail was very proud of his people. They were very smart to give such a fitting name to the mountain.

The boy started his search for his favorite birds. He looked under bushes, in trees, and among the boulders. Like his ancestors, this child of nature was sure-footed as he jumped from one boulder to another. After hours of diligent searching he was at last rewarded. There in a large nest were two downy eaglets.

"My little *napawchick*," he happily exclaimed. He ran his long, slender fingers tenderly over the downy eaglets. Their bright eyes looked up fearlessly at Beaver Tail. They seemed accustomed to his soft voice and gentle touch.

"My own, my own," he said over and over. So happy and proud he was!

Beaver Tail appointed himself their guardian. He would see to it that no harm came to his pets. From that day for many weeks Beaver Tail made faithful visits to his eaglets. He was very careful not to disclose his find to anyone, not even his parents. When the eaglets were old enough he would take them home with him and surprise everyone.

One day the boy decided it was time to bring his eaglets home. He left home very early without telling his mother, for he knew very well she would object to his plan. Beaver Tail was very happy and so excited his thoughts ran in many directions at once.

"I'll soon be wearing eagle feathers in my hair," he

thought. "My arrows will be decorated with them. Little sister, Yellow Flower, will look so pretty with an eagle feather in her hair. Hal Bee will quickly drive away the evil spirits with my eagle feathers. The evil spirits will not dare to hover around."

Then his mother's words suddenly came back to him: "Don't ever help Hal Bee. He does not belong to our clan and he brings illness to us." Beaver Tail shook his head sadly. He was still confused as to why Hal Bee belonged to another clan.

When Beaver Tail reached the top of the rugged mountain he was completely exhausted. For some reason the mountain was harder to climb than on previous trips. His head ached, throbbing like Hal Bee's gourd rattle. His parched lips caused him considerable pain. But worst of all, he could not find the eagle's nest!

"Where's the nest and my little eaglets?" he cried, rubbing his weary eyes. Again he looked around him. The mountain had changed, the sides were higher and steeper. Beaver Tail's heart was full of fear, for he knew he was lost.

"Why are the gods angry with me?" he cried. But his cries were of no avail. The echoes only mocked him. He threw himself down under the shade of a large boulder to think of a way to cope with his strange predicament. He knew he was lost on the high mountain. He must be brave like his people and keep calm. But what to do?

As he lay looking up at the blue sky, his father's advice came to him, "Beaver Tail, if you ever get lost, just lie down and close your eyes. Take a short nap if possible. You'll find it always helps."

"That's what I'll do," Beaver Tail decided and fell into a sound sleep.

He dreamed of the mother eagle swooping down before

him. She ruffled her feathers, stamped her feet, and said very firmly, "Young man, I know how badly you wish to take my little ones, but I shall not let you take them from me. I built my nest on this high mountain that I might raise my young in safety. When I used to build my nests in the valley, your tribe came and carried them away. I've watched you, Beaver Tail, and vowed I'd never let you take them from me. Your people are lovers of birds and take good care of them, but a mother's love is greater. It was I who caused you to be lost on this mountain. But I'll let you go if you will promise to leave my chicks alone."

"I promise never to touch your little chicks again," sobbed Beaver Tail, and just as suddenly as the mother eagle had appeared, she vanished.

Beaver Tail awoke and sat up wondering. Was it only a dream? It seemed so real! He felt hot tears running down his face, but he dried them with his fists, and when he looked around he was relieved to find himself in familiar surroundings. The chirpings of his little feathered friends he plainly heard only a few feet away.

Beaver Tail was almost tempted to step over and touch just once more the silky feathers of his little pets. But a promise is a promise. It was better to return home at once.

As he started the long climb down the mountain, the heart of little Beaver Tail ached with longing for his little pets. But he must take it like a man. Halfway down he stopped to take a last glimpse of his little *napawchick*. The Great Spirit seemed to have compassion for Beaver Tail, for at the same moment the little bright-eyed eaglets peeped over their nest and chirped lustily. "Farewell, Beaver Tail," they seemed to say in their own bird language.

A broad smile of satisfaction lit up the little Pima boy's

handsome face. Beaver Tail looked up to the blue sky and with hands raised he said reverently, "Great Spirit, please, take care of my little eaglets for me."

Gray Arrow Learns a Lesson

GRAY ARROW was a tall, slender twelve-year-old Indian boy. He was very curious to know why his little friend Cottontail always carried a little sack whenever he attended a feast. "Why is he so greedy?" he asked.

Indeed, Cottontail was always one of the first to eat and the last to leave the celebration of feasting and dancing.

"Father, where does Cottontail put all the food he eats?" asked Gray Arrow. "He's not big or fat. And why does he always carry a little sack?"

"Gray Arrow, stop spying on your friend. It's wrong to do so," said his father.

But Gray Arrow had made up his mind to find out why Cottontail was so greedy and why he always carried a little sack. The next time a feast was held, Cottontail came very early. As usual, he was carrying his little sack.

When the food was ready, Cottontail was one of the first to sit down to eat. Determined to satisfy his curiosity, Gray Arrow sat next to Cottontail on the ground. Every now and then Gray Arrow would glance at Cottontail who seemed to know that he was being watched — so he ate the food very slowly.

"I'm so shaky today," said Cottontail, dropping some venison. Actually, he was dropping the food into the little open sack lying at his feet.

When it was time for the feast to end, Cottontail picked up his sack and departed for home. Gray Arrow followed, but Cottontail did not know he was being followed.

Cottontail stopped at a little mud hut in the woods. He opened his little sack and gave the food from it to a little old woman.

Five ragged and hungry-looking children ran out of the round house.

"Cottontail, the food will help us to sleep better tonight. We're so glad you are our friend. Grandmother will be happy to mend your little sack," said the oldest child.

"My little sack is all right. You had better eat the food while it is still warm," said Cottontail.

Filled with shame, Gray Arrow knelt behind some bushes, for at last he had discovered the answer to his questions.

Gray Arrow slowly turned his steps homeward. He could still see the hungry children and hear their small voices. "Cottontail, the food will help us to sleep better tonight," rang in his ears.

Upon his arrival, Gray Arrow told his father his experience.

"Father, I'm so ashamed of myself," he cried, striking his fists together and pacing back and forth.

"My son, never judge anyone until you see his wrongful act," advised his father.

"Believe me, I'll never do it again. I'm going to take some food myself to those children in the woods," promised Gray Arrow, and he started at once to hunt for game with his bow and arrows.

Morning Star and Meteor

ONCE A PRETTY LITTLE ORPHAN, Morning Star, lived with her uncle, Meteor, in the Pima country. She was very industrious and kept their house clean and neat.

Every day Morning Star went to the spring to fetch water in the olla that she carried on her head. It helped her to walk straight and gracefully. When she needed firewood she would take her two-legged burden basket and prop stick and go out to the woods to gather it.

One day Meteor called her to his side under the ramada of long, dry cactus poles covered with willow branches. He said, "I'm growing old and haven't many years to be with you. Morning Star, you are old enough to marry and . . ."

"No, Uncle, I'll never marry!" exclaimed Morning Star, interrupting him. "I want to be the first maiden of our tribe to remain unmarried. Maidens grow old as soon as

107

they marry." With a look of determination she patted her uncle's shoulder. But her real reason for wanting to remain unmarried was to care for this uncle who had been so good to her. Perhaps Meteor knew this. Anyway, from that day her uncle dropped the subject of marriage in speaking to Morning Star. But he continued to think much about it.

"My niece is so beautiful. It is not right she should remain unmarried. The maidens of the village will scorn her," he reasoned sadly.

Morning Star, however, was content to help her uncle, who was growing old and feeble. She went down to the brook and waded in the cool water. She played with the minnows whom she lovingly called "water's green babies," and talked to the birds in the trees.

Whirlwind became her friend and helped unearth small roots which she used as medicine for her uncle. Sometimes she took home long straight arrow-weeds.

"Uncle is an expert arrow-maker, I'll take these arrow-weeds to him. It will make him happy," she said, her black eyes shining with love for her uncle.

One morning the girl arose very early to grind parched corn for their morning meal. She uncovered her *metate* just outside the house. With a little deerskin she wiped it very clean. Placing a handful of corn on the *metate,* she rolled her oblong stone grinder over the kernels, singing as she worked.

Her singing was suddenly interrupted by a young man's voice, "Maiden, I have come to ask your uncle to let me take you home to the Big House to be my bride."

Morning Star looked up from her *metate* and said sternly, "I don't want ever to marry. I'll never desert my aged uncle. Who will grind the corn and prepare his favorite *pinole?*"

The boy took a turquoise necklace from his bearskin pouch and attempted to clasp it around the maiden's neck — the Indian token of marriage.

"I told you I'll never marry — not you or anyone else," she cried, pushing the necklace away.

Her uncle heard her cries and came out from the thatched house.

"Young man, you had better leave now," he ordered. "My niece does not want to marry you." The suitor left, shouting angry words, threatening to tell Chief Antelope.

"He'll send his warriors to slay you," the angry brave shouted.

Before the sun sank behind the big gray mountain nearby, warriors were seen approaching from the east, from the Big House.

"Uncle!" cried Morning Star. "I see that young brave leading the warriors. Run and hide in the woods." But Meteor refused to go. He stayed inside the house until his niece begged again, "Uncle, hear their war-whoops!"

The angry warriors, led by the rejected suitor, arrived shouting, "Meteor, come out. We dare you to come and meet us!"

The uncle heard their commands. And he turned to Morning Star, who was sobbing softly beside him. "My beloved niece, the time has come. Be brave." He straightened his shoulders and bravely walked out to meet the warriors, singing the Pima war song, *"Yoo le va, Yoo le va."* He was willing to sacrifice his life in defense of his niece's honor.

But Morning Star's heavy heart had a similar desire — to protect her uncle. She ran outside and stubbornly stood in front of her uncle just as the enemy started to aim their sharp arrows at Meteor.

109

When they saw the girl's defiant face, daring them to shoot her, they were perplexed at the turn of events.

The boy immediately held a council. He said, "We must not harm the girl. We will go home and return under the cover of darkness. Then we can carry her away to be my bride." And they left for their own village — Casa Grande.

Morning Star led her aged uncle into the house, and comforted him with cheerful words.

"The enemy will never harm us. I'm going to the woods where my friend Whirlwind lives. He'll help us."

"How can Whirlwind help?" asked the Uncle. "You'll see," she answered cheerfully, and started to make herself presentable for her important mission.

Morning Star took out her little bearskin pouch containing red powdered clay and painted her face. From another pouch she took out white powdered clay and with it drew two straight lines across each cheek, on her forehead, and then on her chin. Next she dipped her long slender finger in a tiny pouch containing black, powdered clay, and touched below each eye, causing them to sparkle more brightly, like stars.

Her uncle watched her and proudly decided, "No one is more beautiful than little Morning Star."

Now she was ready to call on Whirlwind of the forest.

When she reached the woods she climbed one of the trees and called Whirlwind by singing softly. Before long the trees were nodding and the leaves rustling. Whirlwind had heard and came at once. He carried Morning Star back to her uncle's house. They held a council while the people of the village were soundly sleeping.

"We must decide before the warriors return," she warned.

"What shall we do? We cannot stay on this land," said the uncle.

"Our friend Whirlwind will take us to the sky where we will remain, to watch and take care of our people. I will help the young maidens. When they see me appear in the morning sky they will know it is time to get up and grind corn for the morning meal," bravely replied the girl.

Her uncle said approvingly, "You are so young but very wise. I will help the men. When they see me shooting across the evening sky they will know the enemy plans to wage war against them. The men will get their bows and arrows ready for the enemy."

So Whirlwind carried them to the sky to shine always for the people below. Since then the Pima Indians look up to the stars with gratitude and recall this beautiful legend.